THE TABERNACLE AND THE OFFERINGS

THE TABERNACLE AND THE OFFERINGS

by

ALBERT LECKIE

PRECIOUS SEED PUBLICATIONS

First published April 2012

ISBN 978-1-871642-44-5

Printed in China

Contents

FOREWORD

A few words regarding the fact that this book is being published more than twenty years after Albert Leckie was called home to be with the Lord might help the reader to appreciate its contents and format.

For nearly thirty years Mr. Leckie conducted the Trimsaran Bible Readings in south west Wales. These were held in August each year and proved to be helpful to many believers in their understanding of a wide range of truth. In 1980 the Readings were devoted to the study of the tabernacle. Tape recordings of these Bible Readings have become available within the last few years. These have been transcribed and edited into a form suitable for publication and this book is the result. An edited transcript of ministry given elsewhere by Mr. Leckie on the Levitical offerings has also been included.

This book contains many glorious themes of truth in respect of the person and work of our Lord Jesus Christ that will remind an older generation of the rich ministry enjoyed from our brother and establish younger believers in the faith once for all delivered to us. Because of the way the book has been prepared it has not been possible to include any bibliography or references. It is unlikely that everything in this book is original but the reader will discover delightful lines of truth not commonly expressed elsewhere.

Strenuous efforts have been made to discover the whereabouts of our brother's notes, particularly those bound in Oxford Loose Leaf Bible covers, but they have not been successful. A plea is made that if their whereabouts are known they be made available to assist in future publications.

The publishers are grateful to John Bennett for editing and proof reading the manuscript and for the wholehearted encouragement of Mr. Leckie's sister, Mrs. Winnie Lee, in the work of committing her brother's oral ministry to print.

May the Lord be pleased to use these notes on the tabernacle and the offerings to the blessing of the Lord's people, that there might be a deeper understanding of our Saviour's person and work and a greater devotion to Him.

Ian Jackson
Eastbourne
November 2011

Introduction

The importance of the tabernacle

We live in a day when there are those who would dismiss the tabernacle as being no more than Israel's place of worship in the wilderness but it becomes clear in the New Testament that there was more to it than that. In Hebrews, frequent reference is made to the tabernacle. It was a 'shadow of heavenly things', 8. 5, a 'figure for the time then present', 9. 9, and the 'patterns of things in the heavens', 9. 23. Much importance is thus attached to the tabernacle.

The details of the tabernacle were given around 1,500 years before Christ and they are full of His glory. It becomes most interesting and, indeed, soul thrilling to observe as we study the tabernacle that the type is fulfilled in the antitype and that the figures have now become fact.

We do well to remember the word of the Lord Jesus. In John chapter 5, He spoke of the Old Testament scriptures as being, 'they which testify of me'. Thus, if we only had that verse, we would have good grounds for seeing in the tabernacle a picture of Christ. Further, we are told that speaking to two disciples on the Emmaus road He unfolded to them 'in all the scriptures the things concerning himself', Luke 24. 27. Addressing Himself to the Jews, Jesus said, 'had ye believed Moses, ye would have believed me: for he wrote of me', John 5. 46. Moses wrote Exodus and the other books of the Pentateuch; Jesus said that he wrote concerning Him. The real value in studying the tabernacle is to see Christ in it.

Standing on the wilderness side of the Red Sea, Israel had an occasion to rejoice in the power of God. The taskmasters, their enemies, had been judged by God but now a greater experience awaited them. This was the experience of the presence of God amongst them. To know God's presence surpasses any experience of His power. To have been delivered from Egypt and to have seen the Red Sea swallow up their enemies was no doubt an unforgettable experience. In the song of Exodus chapter 15, however, they desire something greater than the overthrow of their enemies. Moses sang, 'He is my God, and I will prepare him an habitation', v. 2. His desire was that he might know God's presence amongst His people.

Everything required for this habitation was given willingly by the people; nothing was exacted from them. A willing-hearted people gave the materials and a wise-hearted people set to work.

Nothing in connection with the tabernacle was left to the imagination or the discretion of Moses. Numerous times in Exodus, Moses was commanded to see that the tabernacle was made according to the pattern that God showed him in the mount. There is some significance in this. In Exodus chapters 25-27, we have the divine command to Moses regarding the tabernacle; in chapters 36-38, the people are told exactly what God had commanded. You will discover that there are ninety-eight verses in chapters 25-27 and the same number of verses in chapters 36-38. Thus, all was carried out in detail according to the pattern.

Divine order

In a broad way, three great truths are brought before us which present divine order in God's dealings with men. These are: salvation; sanctification; and service. Approaching the tabernacle, one was confronted with a wall of white linen. It was about nine feet high, too high for a man to look over. It was a symbol of that holiness which kept man on the outside. If one desired to enter in, there was one way, through the gate on the east side. The first thing encountered then was the brazen altar where the sacrifices were killed and where the blood was sprinkled on the horns of the altar and poured out at its base. This speaks of salvation by blood.

Proceeding further, one came to the brazen laver. There, the priests washed their hands and feet, something they did repeatedly. This speaks of sanctification by water. In John chapter

13, the Lord Jesus speaks only of feet washing, but the priests had also to wash their hands. The difference is simply that in the Old Testament the priests had to wash their hands because they repeatedly killed the sacrifices and sprinkled their blood. Our sacrifice, however, was made once for all; it needs no repetition. Accordingly, only our feet need washing and that because of defilement by the way.

Then, leaving the brazen altar and the brazen laver, the priest would enter the holy place. There, he would daily attend the golden altar and the golden lampstand and every Sabbath would change the shewbread on the table of shewbread. The high priest would, on one day each year, the Day of Atonement, enter the holiest of all with incense and blood. This speaks of service for God. Thus, there is divine order in salvation, sanctification and service.

John's Gospel has a tabernacle setting. In John chapter 1 verse 14, 'the word became flesh and tabernacled amongst us' RV margin. Reference is made to the brazen altar, when, in chapter 12, our Saviour said, 'And I, if I be lifted up from the earth, will draw all men unto me'. In chapter 13, reference is made to the brazen laver, when our Saviour said to Simon Peter, 'If I wash thee not, thou hast no part with me'. In chapters 14-16, there is that which answers to the holy place, while, in chapter 17, we enter the holiest of all, the divine presence.

God's habitation

As we think of the tabernacle as God's habitation among His people, it is interesting to remember that as God moved in creation in the six days in Genesis chapter 1, He was not only forming a place where men would dwell but a place where men would commune with Him. What a wonderful thought that God should desire to be with men and to commune with them! In course of time, man had to be driven out of God's presence because of sin but we come to the tabernacle and the Temple on the ground of redemption. On that ground, God dwelt with the nation of Israel but, because of their apostasy and, ultimately, their rejection of Christ, God no longer dwells with that nation. Upon being rejected by the nation, our Saviour said, 'Your house is left unto you desolate', Matt. 23. 38. Today, on the ground of redemption, God dwells with His church and so we have the beautiful language of 2 Corinthians chapter 6 verse 16, 'Ye are the temple of the living God; as God hath said, I will dwell in them, and walk in them; and I will be their God, and they shall be my people'. Let us not forget that God will not be diverted from His original design to dwell with men. This is going to be realized in the day of eternity, the eternal state, when, in the new heavens and the new earth, the tabernacle of God shall be with men, 'and he will dwell with them, and they shall be his people, and God himself shall be with them, and be their God', Rev. 21. 3. I mention this that we might appreciate God's desire to dwell with men.

In connection with this it is interesting to observe the desire of our Saviour when He was here to be in the midst of His people. He gives expression to this over and over again. In John chapter 18, Jesus passed over the brook Cedron with His disciples into a garden; 'And Judas also, which betrayed him, knew the place: for Jesus ofttimes resorted thither with his disciples', 18. 2. It was the custom of our Lord Jesus to take His disciples aside into this garden of Gethsemane to have them there around Himself. After His resurrection, on two occasions, he appeared in the midst of His own in the upper room, even though the doors were shut. He must be with His disciples and He shows them His hands and His side and, in Luke chapter 24, His hands and His feet.

I love the words of 2 Thessalonians chapter 2 verse 1 when the apostle speaks of the Lord's coming. 'Now we beseech you, brethren, by the coming of our Lord Jesus Christ, and by our gathering together unto him'. What a day that shall be when, at His coming again, the purpose for which He died shall be realized and all His people shall be gathered unto Him in the very domain of the enemy.

He dwells with His people today. 'Where two or three are gathered together in my name, there am I in the midst of them', Matt. 18. 20. He has that place where He dwells today, where there are those who gather into His name.

Some comparisons

We may compare the tabernacle with the Temple. The desire which issued in the building of the Temple began with David. He said, 'I will not give sleep to mine eyes, or slumber to mine eyelids, until I find out a place for the Lord, an habitation for the mighty God of Jacob', Ps. 132. 4-5. Paul, at Antioch in Pisidia, spoke of David as a man after God's own heart and this was true, especially in the sense that He knew God's desire to dwell with His people. In respect of the tabernacle, however, there is a fulfilment of a desire to that originated in the heart of God Himself, to dwell among His people. 'Let them make me a sanctuary; that I may dwell among them', Exod. 25. 8.

We may also compare the tabernacle with creation. There is one chapter in Genesis devoted to creation but in Exodus fifteen chapters are devoted to the erection of the tabernacle. Details of the tabernacle are repeated seven times over and it is remarkable that God does this. They are given first in the details God gave to Moses. These are then repeated in the commandments Moses gave to Bezaleel and Aholiab. The details are then given to the nation and repeated when the materials are collected, when the tabernacle is finished, at the placing of the vessels and when the tabernacle is ultimately reared. God repeats this information because the tabernacle speaks of Christ; God never tires of Him. If we could see our Lord in the tabernacle we too would never tire of the details.

Furthermore, God made the world in which we live, suitable for habitation, in six days. The tabernacle was nine and one half months in building. 'The heavens declare the glory of God; and the firmament sheweth his handywork', Ps. 19. 1. The word for 'God' here is *Elohim*, the heavens declare the glory of the creator

God. In Psalm 29, however, in speaking about the tabernacle, the psalmist says, 'Worship the Lord in the beauty of holiness'. A marginal reading of the verse says, 'Worship Jehovah in His glorious sanctuary', v. 2. The psalmist goes on to say in verse 9, 'In his temple doth every one speak of his glory'. This may be rendered, 'Every whit of it uttereth His glory'. David is not speaking here of the Temple, of course, for it was not built but he speaks of the tabernacle. Thus, the heavens declare the glory of *Elohim*, the creator; but in the tabernacle every whit of it utters *Jehovah*'s glory. After all, in creation the unregenerate man might see the glory of a creator God but one needs covenant relations with God to appreciate the glory of *Jehovah* in the tabernacle.

Measurements in the tabernacle

In the tabernacle all the measurements are taken from the human body, whether it be cubits or the span of the hand breadth. We learn that in the tabernacle we have truth that is infinite brought down to finite understanding. That is important to observe. Reference has been made to the fact that the tabernacle is a 'pattern(s) of things in the heavens', Heb. 9. 23. In the tabernacle, then, such things are brought down to human understanding. In 2 Corinthians chapter 12, the apostle Paul speaks of being caught up into Paradise and hearing unspeakable words not lawful for a man to utter. Paul was not saying he was not able to utter them but that he was not permitted to do so. What Paul saw and heard was not suited to mortal ears, or for this world where mortals live. It touches things beyond finite understanding. In the tabernacle such truth is brought down to human understanding and thus the measurements are taken from the human body.

Note also the recurrence of the half cubit. There are, perhaps, two reasons why these are mentioned. Firstly, the Son of God said of Himself, 'No man knoweth the Son but the Father', Matt. 11. 27. When we touch things in respect of the Son we touch what is inscrutable. Only the Father knows the Son; we shall never be able to know Him fully. Secondly, the tabernacle belonged to the wilderness. In the wilderness we can never acquire full knowledge. Wilderness knowledge is partial and wilderness experience is marked by a limited apprehension. It reminds us of the language of the queen of Sheba when she said to Solomon, 'It was a true report which I heard in mine own land of thine acts, and of thy wisdom: howbeit I believed not their words, until I came, and mine eyes had seen it: and, behold, the one half of the greatness of thy wisdom was not told me: for thou exceedest the fame that I heard', 2 Chr. 9. 5-6. When, at last, we are in His presence (and what a moment that shall be) and we gaze on His glory, we shall also say, 'The half hath not been told'.

Bezaleel and Aholiab

The pattern was given to Moses but the construction of the tabernacle was put in the hands of Bezaleel and Aholiab, Exod. 31. 1-11. This work was not given to them because they were descendants of Tubalcain, who was 'an instructer of every artificer in brass and iron', Gen. 4. 22, though this might have been expected to be the case because of all the work involved in copper, silver and gold. In fact, the skill required was much more than natural or inherited skill and what is emphasized about these men is that their skill was something which, in a particular way, was divinely given.

This becomes clear when the Lord says to Moses, 'See, I have called by name Bezaleel the son of Uri, the son of Hur, of the tribe of Judah: and I have filled him with the spirit of God, in wisdom, and in understanding, and in knowledge, and in all manner of workmanship', Exod. 31. 2-3. When we come to consider the golden lampstand or the mercy seat, each beaten out of one piece of pure gold, ornamented as they were, there is not a man born that could do that with merely natural skill. Rather, there was divinely given wisdom. There are lessons in this for the present day. There is the serious danger, even in assembly life, that there is an emphasis put on natural skill and wisdom in things pertaining to what is spiritual, that which requires divine wisdom. This is where Corinth went astray.

Furthermore, names in the Old Testament have vital significance. Bezaleel was the son of Uri, the son of Hur, Exod. 31. 2. Here was the man raised up by God to supervise the construction of the tabernacle. Bezaleel, 'under the shadow of God', directs us to one who knew much of God's presence and protection. The meaning of Uri, 'light of Jehovah', seems almost paradoxical to the meaning of Bezaleel but it is, in fact, under the shadow of God that light is imparted. Hur means 'noble' and 'white' and points to the nobility and righteousness of his character and ways. These are the qualities God looks for: men who know something of His presence and protection, who enjoy the divine light of heavenly communication and who, as to their character and ways, are noble and white. God will not trust His work to anybody.

Aholiab was the son of Ahisamach, Exod. 31. 6. Aholiab, 'tent of my father', indicates that his character and ways had been developed by association with his father. Ahisamach, 'brotherly support', indicates that he enjoyed the fellowship and support of his brethren. There is a great lesson to be learned today regarding this. We have almost come to a time when everything orthodox has been thrown overboard and all that has been taught down the years is out of date and old fashioned. There is a tendency to reject what has been taught by our fathers and assemblies are all the worse for it. The rejection of our fathers' ways, teaching and character has spelt disaster in many assemblies today. It is important for the young to develop their ways from the spiritual character of the men who went before them.

Observe the tribes from which they came. Bezaleel came from the tribe of Judah and Aholiab from Dan, Exod. 31. 2, 6. This is significant in that in the order of the tribes whilst journeying through the wilderness Judah was the first and Dan the last. Thus, God chose from Judah the first and Dan the last to make it apparent that the whole nation was involved in this matter. It is all too possible that we can think that we can only be helped by the mighty men of Judah and the lowly men of Dan are neglected. Spiritual prosperity can only be enjoyed where there is an acknowledgement of the sovereign liberty of the Holy Spirit to use whomsoever He will. Our God is the God of the unexpected. Very often today, human arrangement and discretion has shut out the sovereign liberty of the Spirit so that we have the recurrence of 1 Corinthians chapter 12, the head saying to the feet, 'I have no need of you'. This could not be said in the tabernacle. God took one from the head, Bezaleel, and one from the feet, Aholiab.

'As the dew of Hermon, and as the dew that descended upon the mountains of Zion: for there the Lord commanded the blessing, even life for evermore', Ps. 133. 3. The expression 'and as the dew' is in italics and so the verse really reads, 'As the dew of Hermon that descended upon the mountains of Zion'. There were not two dews: the same dew, copious in its descent, fell on Mount Hermon and on Mount Zion. Hermon is in the north and Zion is in the south. Encamped around northerly Hermon were the lowly tribes of Dan, Naphtali and Issachar, but encamped around the southerly Zion was the mighty tribe of Judah. As the dew that fell on the lowly tribe and the mighty tribe, there the Lord commanded the blessing. There is blessing where it is recognized that the Holy Spirit can operate not only on the mighty but also on the lowly. When God wanted an apostle to the circumcision, He called a Peter from the fishing nets; when He wanted an apostle to the uncircumcision, He called a Saul of Tarsus from the feet of Gamaliel. This is how God works; fishermen and learned men, mighty and lowly, Judah and Dan, Bezaleel and Aholiab.

The materials

There was no legal demand for the materials and they had to be given from a willing heart. The amazing thing was that they needed to be restrained. In fact, it is recorded that the people brought 'much more than enough for the service of the work, which the Lord commanded to make', Exod. 35. 5, but though they gave so liberally the gold, silver and copper was all weighed, 38. 24, 25, 29. What we give is weighed in the divine balance. It is said of Mary's ointment that it was a pound of spikenard, very costly. This is the divine assessment of Mary's gift; we shall learn

Introduction

at the judgment seat of Christ the divine assessment of what we give and therefore we are encouraged to give with liberality.

The people had, of course, just been delivered from Egypt. Therefore, it is evident that the material, perhaps with the exception of the wood that grew in the wilderness, came from Egypt. The command of the Lord had been, 'Let every man borrow of his neighbour, and every woman of her neighbour, jewels of silver, and jewels of gold', Exod. 11. 2. It was from these that the tabernacle was made. The word 'borrow' is, strictly speaking, 'demand'. This was not just because the fear of God was on the Egyptians but there were wages that were their due for long years of servitude and slavery. Accordingly, the tabernacle was not built of borrowed materials but of wages that they demanded.

In Exodus chapter 32 we have the occasion of the golden calf. This calf was made from those same wages. Gold given for the calf was lost to the tabernacle. In fact, it was completely lost because the gold of which the calf was made was ground to powder. Some who devote time, interest and energy to some particular idol fail to appreciate that by so doing they are robbing God and robbing the assembly and that to both their present and eternal loss.

There was one exception to the voluntary giving. The silver in the tabernacle was demanded; produced by the commandment of God. From twenty years old and upward they had to give an offering unto the Lord. 'The rich shall not give more, and the poor shall not give less than half a shekel', Exod. 30. 15. Thus, they were enjoined to give of their silver and this was in fact the ransom money. It speaks of redemption. The best need Christ and, praise God, he suffices for the worst. Here, then, is the only 'must' in respect of the materials for the tabernacle and it is that which speaks of the saving work of Christ, that which formed the foundation of the tabernacle proper.

18

Some broad details of the tabernacle

It was in the tabernacle structure proper where God Himself dwelt. This was of boards which were each ten cubits high and one and one half cubits wide. Each stood up on a foundation of silver and were all held together by five bars. The boards were made of wood and were overlaid with gold.

Over these boards, once erected, were placed the ten curtains of fine twined linen, blue, purple and scarlet. These were coupled together in interesting fashion. Then, over these ten curtains were thrown eleven other curtains. These too were coupled together. They were made of goat's hair and they formed a covering for the beautiful curtains. Over these were coverings of rams' skins dyed red and on top of these were badgers' skins. There were two sets of curtains and two coverings. All of this we shall find to be most interesting.

The tabernacle proper was divided into two compartments by a beautiful vail. These compartments are defined for us as 'the holy place' and 'the holiest' or 'the holy of holies'. There were three vessels in the holy place: the golden altar; the golden lampstand; and the table of shewbread. Every morning the golden lampstand had to have its wick taken away and be dressed. The golden lampstand illuminated the holy place, providing necessary light for the priest at the golden altar, as he changed the loaves on the table of shewbread every Sabbath.

In the holiest was the ark in which were the two tables of the covenant. The lid of the ark was the mercy seat, which was made of pure gold with cherubim whose wings touched and whose faces looked down. It was there that God dwelt and there that He communed with His people. In fact, it only became a mercy seat once the blood was sprinkled on it. It was on the basis of sprinkled blood that the throne of God itself became a mercy seat; on that ground alone could God meet with His people and commune with them.

Later in Israel's history, there was an incident when the men of Bethshemesh took the lid off the ark and looked in. The result was that many were slain. This was a dreadful tragedy for simply looking into the ark. That is very often interpreted as meaning that we should not be inquisitive as far as the person of Christ is concerned. It is true that there are details of His person which are beyond our investigation but that is not, strictly speaking, the interpretation of that event. They were slain because once the lid was taken off the ark and they looked into it they came face to face with the unbroken tables of the covenant. No mere, mortal, sinful man could see them and live. The unbroken tables must slay him. However, God was pleased to dwell in the midst of His people when these unbroken tables were covered and blood was sprinkled on that covering.

In addition to the tabernacle structure proper there were the hangings of the court. These formed the perimeter wall of the tabernacle itself. This, in fact, would have been the first to be seen by an outsider when he approached the tabernacle. The perimeter wall was made of pillars. We are not told the material from which they were made but each was five cubits high. Each rested on a foundation of copper, in contrast with the boards of the tabernacle proper which rested on a foundation of silver. Each was held in place by pins and cords. The cords were attached to the pillar and secured to the ground by means of pins, like tent pegs. Furthermore, the pillars were joined together by fillets, or connecting rods made of silver. On the pillars, by means of hooks, were hung what are called the 'hangings of fine twined linen'. The hoops were made of silver and the hangings were suspended on them.

Within the perimeter walls was a court. Here was the brazen altar and the brazen laver. Blood is connected with the altar and water with the brazen laver. Our Saviour's side was pierced and forthwith came there out blood (the altar) and water (the laver). In the altar we have salvation, at the laver sanctification and in the holy place service. This, of course, is God's order. We shall also see that in the tabernacle proper there is a beautiful picture of the assembly as a habitation of God through the Spirit and in that white perimeter wall a beautiful picture of the assembly in its testimony manward. It is true that every whit of it uttereth His glory: either His personal glory or His glory as seen in His saints. Here is both precious and practical truth.

In the book of Numbers, the tribes all camp in relation to the tabernacle. They only moved with the cloud and their whole life revolved around the dwelling place of God. The secret of the spiritual prosperity of any assembly today is the whole life revolving around God's dwelling place and moving only when the cloud moves.

The ordering of the camp

Before the gate through which one had to enter the camp were encamped Moses and Aaron. They were the nearest. Next nearest were the Levites, with the Kohathites encamped on the south, the Merarites on the north and the Gershonites on the west. The Kohathites had responsibility for carrying the vessels of the tabernacle, the Merarites for carrying the boards and sockets and the Gershonites for carrying the soft materials.

The Levites were numbered twice. Whereas the children of Israel were numbered at aged twenty, the Levites were numbered at one month old and at age thirty. They then served until the age of fifty. They were numbered twice because they were men who had a special duty and service for God. The apostle Paul was like that. In Galatians chapter 1 verse 4, he speaks about God, 'who separated me from my mother's womb'; he was, as it were, numbered at one month. Then, he was later called on the Damascus road.

After the Levites, there were the twelve tribes, the common people as distinct from the priests and the Levites. On the east were Judah, Issachar and Zebulon; on the west were Ephraim, Manasseh and Benjamin whilst on the north (as one would expect, for it always speaks of judgement) were Dan, Asher and

Naphtali. On the south were Reuben, Simeon and Gad. They were gathered according to the standard of their particular grouping. Judah had his standard, as did Ephraim and Dan and Reuben.

The meaning of the tribes' names is fascinating.

East side	Judah means 'praise'
	Issachar means 'hire'
	Zebulon means 'dwelling of rest'
West side	Ephraim means 'fruitful'
	Manasseh means 'forgetting'
	Benjamin means 'son of my right hand'
North side	Dan means 'judging'
	Asher means 'happy'
	Naphtali means 'wrestling' or 'stirring'
South side	Reuben means 'see, a son'
	Simeon means 'hearing'
	Gad means 'a troop' or 'the power of God'

Encamped around the tabernacle they were protected from the sun by the pillar of cloud and given light by night by the pillar of fire. Thus, their entire need was met. There is a practical lesson we may learn from this. As their whole life revolved around the tabernacle they were blessed and so it is in our day. It used to be the case that the saints lived for God and the assembly. Lives were ordered in relation to the assembly and they got their priorities right in the light of the sanctuary. If they wanted a house to live in they would preferably get it nearer to the place of meeting than their place of employment. If the assembly would be affected by their absence they would either forego or rearrange their holidays. They would sooner be late to work than to the meeting. If there was a choice to be made there was no question with them as to what should be first. How far removed we are from this today.

Then, generally, the placing of the tribes in order around the tabernacle, reminds us that our God is a God of order. This has always been true of God. We may be reminded of the words of

Moses when he said, 'What nation is there so great, who hath God so nigh unto them?' Deut. 4. 7. They had God's presence in their midst, which struck terror into the hearts of their enemies. They were not encamped around the tabernacle to protect it but by keeping themselves around the tabernacle they were protected.

It has been left to tradition to tell us the emblem on each of their standards. Judah's was a lion, Ephraim's was an ox, Dan's was the eagle and Reuben's a man. Each of these speak of Christ in His varied glories. Whenever the tents were pitched, the standards were set up and every Israelite rallied to his particular standard. In this hostile world we should know our place in respect to the assembly and give Christ His rightful place as ordered by God. When that is true we shall know God's presence; and there men shall realize that they can meet with God when they know God is amongst them of a truth.

The Levites were consecrated to the service of the tabernacle. They were not required to go to war. They not only served in the holy things but the silver trumpets were entrusted to them. Accordingly, among the twelve tribes there were the warriors, numbered for warfare, the workers, the Levites who carried the vessels, and the worshippers, the priests. Today, God's people are warriors, workers, and worshippers.

Balaam looked down on the camp, possibly extending over ten square miles, in order and covered by the cloud of God's presence, and he said, 'How goodly are thy tents, O Jacob, and thy tabernacles, O Israel!' Num. 24. 5. Would to God that our God could find such order in His assemblies today!

The Tabernacle proper and the Court
Exodus 26. 15-30; Exodus 27. 9-18

We may think of the tabernacle and the court of the tabernacle in a two-fold way. Firstly, we may see in the tabernacle proper a picture of the assembly as the habitation of God through the Spirit; the assembly in its God-ward aspect. Secondly, we may see in the court and its hangings of fine twined linen a picture of the assembly in its testimony man-ward. As we consider this we shall see, of course, in a paramount way the glories of the Lord Jesus Christ. In the tabernacle there are not only presented to us His personal glories but also His glories as reflected in His people and in His own work.

The tabernacle proper

The boards   The tabernacle proper was constructed of forty-eight boards. There were twenty boards each on the north and south sides, vv. 18, 20, and eight boards on the west side, v. 22. These eight boards on the west side consisted of six boards and two corner boards which strengthened the structure. They were coupled beneath and above the head of it by two rings. It is interesting to observe that in his epistles, not in the KJV but in the Greek text, Paul uses the expression 'in Christ Jesus' exactly forty-eight times. We shall see how beautifully this fits as we think of boards of acacia wood, overlaid with gold, standing up in the presence of God.

Each board was made of shittim, or acacia, wood, 26. 15, and each was overlaid with gold, 26. 29. Acacia wood grew in the desert. In scripture, wood always speaks of humanity. Acacia wood does not speak of incorruptible humanity, as is often taught, because it applies to believers today. The ark was made of acacia wood and there it speaks of humanity, as it does here in the boards, but with the distinction that when wood speaks of the humanity of Christ it is His unique humanity that is in view; here it is just humanity.

25

The boards were overlaid with gold. There are occasions where reference is made to 'pure gold' but here it is simply to 'gold'. Pure gold speaks of deity but gold speaks of divine righteousness. There are three occurrences of the word Godhead in the New Testament but it is not the same Greek word each time.

'For in him dwelleth all the fulness of the Godhead bodily', Col. 2. 9.

'For the invisible things of him from the creation of the world are clearly seen, being understood by the things that are made, even his eternal power and Godhead; so that they are without excuse', Rom. 1. 20.

'Forasmuch then as we are the offspring of God, we ought not to think that the Godhead is like unto gold, or silver, or stone, graven by art and man's device', Acts 17. 29.

When it is Christ, it is deity in view, Col. 2. 9. When it is creation, it is a declaration of that which pertains to deity, Rom. 1. 20; Acts 17. 29. 'Pure gold' speaks of deity; 'gold' speaks of what pertains to deity, divine righteousness. The boards, speaking of the believer, could not therefore be covered with pure gold because we are never clothed with deity nor do we partake of it. We are partakers of the divine nature but we shall never partake of deity.

Gold speaks of divine righteousness and a beautiful picture is presented. Here is fallen man standing in the presence of God, clothed in divine righteousness, as a result of having received, without reserve, the person of Christ and His redemptive work. 'But now the righteousness of God without the law is manifested, being witnessed by the law and the prophets; even the righteousness of God which is by faith of Jesus Christ unto all and upon all them that believe', Rom. 3. 21-22. That the righteousness of God is 'upon all' them that believe is seen in the boards overlaid with gold. Grasp the wonder of it all!

The righteousness of Christ is invariably used in connection with His own righteousness. The Bible does not teach that we are clothed in the righteousness of Christ; His personal righteousness is never imputed to anyone. It is the righteousness of God that is imputed. The righteousness of God is viewed in a two-fold way; each reference is either to God's character or to a righteousness that He provides. In every instance, one needs to decide of which the writer is speaking. When He speaks of the righteousness of God 'unto all', He speaks of a means of being right with God. This means of being right with God is 'unto' all in its direction. It is offered to all, because of propitiation. It is 'upon all' them that believe, as a shelter from the storm, because of substitution. God offers to all this means of being right with Him and it is upon all them that believe.

Each board had two tenons, v. 17. The word 'tenon' means 'hand' and so each of these boards had two hands. Thus, there were forty-eight boards with ninety-six tenons or hands. Verse 17 also tells us that each board was set in order. The margin of the Newberry Bible indicates 'they were made parallel to each other'. The New Translation (JND) says they were 'connected one to the other'. Each board was therefore made parallel to and connected to the other. Furthermore, we learn that each board rested on two sockets of silver, vv. 19-25. The silver came from the redemption money. Counting the four sockets for the pillars of the beautiful vail, the foundation of the tabernacle was one hundred sockets of silver. Each of these sockets of silver weighed one talent, 38. 27. It is understood that each talent weighs about one hundredweight and thus the tabernacle rested on about five tons of silver. This was an amazing foundation.

The two tenons or hands on each board grasped two sockets of silver and, by reason of this, the boards stood up. Here we have a picture of the believer, rather than Christ Himself. The believer is now standing in the presence of God. As sinners, we were fallen men yet, by God's grace, we now have a standing in the divine presence. 'If thou, Lord, shouldest mark iniquities, O Lord, who shall stand?' Ps. 130. 3. None of us could stand up to examination in the divine court of justice. That justice must smite us all, but now, by His grace, we stand.

The tenons grasping the two sockets of silver is a beautiful picture of our salvation. What has enabled us to have this standing in divine grace is the fact that our two hands have grasped the silver. The silver, of course, speaks of the atonement as it came from the ransom money which had been collected for the service of the tabernacle, 30. 10. There were two hands, or tenons, and the idea is that they accepted, without reserve or qualification, the redemptive work of Christ. It is this alone that gives a man a standing in God's presence. It is not that one hand accepts the work of Christ and the other rests on something else just in case one might fail and the other succeed. That would never give a fallen man a standing in the presence of God. He must accept with both hands. Trying Jesus does not save; *trusting* Jesus does save.

Two thoughts are worthy of our notice, often helpful in explaining to the unsaved the way of salvation. Two hands receive the silver and by reason of receiving the silver the boards rested upon the silver. Here are two aspects of salvation. We receive Christ and we rest upon Christ. When John speaks of the way of salvation he always uses the Greek preposition '*eis*', which means 'into'. 'Whosoever believeth *into* Him shall not perish', John 3. 16. However, when Peter and Paul speak of salvation they always employ the Greek preposition '*epi*', which means 'upon'. 'Believe *upon* the Lord Jesus Christ, and thou shalt be saved', Acts 16. 31. Peter, quoting from Isaiah chapter 28, where the prophet is speaking of Christ as the tried stone and sure foundation, says, 'He that believeth *upon* him shall not be confounded', 1 Peter 2. 6. Two hands receiving the silver speaks of believing *into* and the boards resting upon the silver speaks of believing *upon*; and the proof of receiving by faith is that one rests by faith. If one receives by faith without reserve or qualification then one rests by faith upon what has been received by faith. So there are two sides to salvation: receiving and resting.

The boards are considered together rather than individually. They were standing up together and held together. This is the idea of it being a habitation of God by the Spirit. It is what is collective that is in view rather than that which is individual. It is individuals together collectively viewed as a habitation of God through the Spirit. The church as the body of Christ is a mystery hidden in the heart of God from the beginning of the world but there are many types of the church in the Old Testament. Ephesians chapter 5 makes it clear that Eve is a picture of the church. 'For this cause shall a man leave his father and mother, and shall be joined unto his wife, and they two shall be one flesh. This is a great mystery: but I speak concerning Christ and the church', Eph. 5. 31-32. The Gentile brides of Joseph and Moses speak of the church and Hebrews chapter 3 verse 5 makes it plain that even the tabernacle was a type of the church. Moses was faithful in all God's house, referring to the tabernacle. Then, it says, 'Whose house are we', Heb. 3. 6.

What glory there is in these boards! The glory of His redemptive work, the glory of the result of it, our standing in divine righteousness is a reflection of the glory of the person and work of our Lord Jesus Christ.

The boards not only rested on silver but they were held together by bars. The middle bar on each side of the tabernacle passed from end to end. The bars were made of shittim wood overlaid with gold and were held in place by rings of gold. There is a little controversy regarding the bars. There were five bars on the north side, five on the south side and five on the west side, fifteen in all. There is distinction in one of the bars. 'The middle bar in the midst of the boards shall reach from end to end', v. 28, or pass through. We have to decide whether this means that it actually slotted through a hole that was made in all the standing boards and was therefore hidden or that the other four bars did not go right to the end in contrast to the middle one. I tend to the thought of shooting through; the middle bar was shot through and was hidden. I know that there are those who would tell us that this would make the boards too wide, we are not told the width, but I

29

do not think that is the case. Four bars were seen and the middle bar that shot through was hidden.

Keeping this still in relation to the assembly being a habitation of God through the Spirit, the five bars signify the five gifts of Ephesians chapter 4. 'And he gave some, apostles; and some, prophets; and some, evangelists; and some, pastors and teachers', v. 11. I know that there are those who would tell us that the hidden bar refers to the Holy Spirit but that must, of course, be ruled out because all these bars were made of wood overlaid with gold. The wood speaks of humanity and so the unseen bar cannot be the Holy Spirit for He never assumed humanity.

The evangelist is the hidden bar for the simple reason that the sphere of the evangelist is not in the house or the assembly. He hears the commission 'go' but nevertheless he works with the assembly in view and the results of his work will be seen there. He is not seen, but the effect of his work is seen. That is why there is no mention of the gift of the evangelist in 1 Corinthians chapters 12-14. There, it is the operation of the gifts in the sphere of the assembly. That is not the sphere of the evangelist's work. Nevertheless, as much as the other gifts, the evangelist does have a part to play in the perfecting of the saints, in that he works with this in view.

These bars were held together by *rings of gold*. 'And thou shalt overlay the boards with gold, and make their rings of gold for places for the bars: and thou shalt overlay the bars with gold', Exod. 26. 29. This is an important matter as well. Gifts given by the ascended Christ are divinely upheld. In Revelation chapters 1 and 2, He is the one who holds the seven stars in His right hand. Accordingly, the gifts are divinely given and divinely upheld.

As far as the *dimensions* are concerned, each of these boards was ten cubits high and one and one-half cubits broad, v. 16. The tabernacle proper was therefore thirty cubits long, ten cubits high and ten cubits wide. The width was made up of six boards measuring one and one-half cubits in width (making nine cubits) and the other cubit was made up by the two corner boards (angled as they were) each furnishing half a cubit to the width of the tabernacle.

The number ten speaks of responsibility. Responsible man falls before the law but the redeemed man stands up in the presence of God. Our responsibility has been met in the death of Christ and so we stand before God. The relationship of the redeemed man to the law is brought before us in Romans chapter 8. God's Son condemned sin in the flesh 'that the righteousness (righteous requirement) of the law might be fulfilled in us'. In our unconverted days we could not keep the law; it was set before us as the principle by which a man ought to live, but we could not help but break it. It was weak through the flesh, but now we are no longer after the flesh but after the Spirit, and the righteous requirements of the law are fulfilled not by us but *in* us, without us being aware of it.

The pins and cords

The tabernacle had pins and cords, 35. 18, a fact that is sometimes omitted when the tabernacle is considered. There were pins and cords for the court and for the tabernacle. These cords were fixed to the tabernacle structure by being thrown over it from the north to the south. They were attached on the north side by a pin for each cord and similarly on the south side. This would not only give security to the structure but support to the curtains and the coverings, keeping them from sagging as they formed the roof of the tabernacle. The cords would afford a suspension.

The curtains

The curtains were of blue, purple, scarlet, and fine twined linen. Over them were the goats' hair curtains, then the rams' skins dyed red, and on top of that the badgers' skins. Thus, the roof of the tabernacle, as seen from the inside, was the beautiful curtains of blue, scarlet, and fine twined linen. All that was seen from the outside was the badgers' skins. As the priest moved in the holy place by the light of the golden lampstand, he would see the beautiful gold of the boards and above him the blue, purple, scarlet and fine twined linen. As he moved in the holiest on the Day of Atonement, the glory of the Shekinah there illuminated that beautiful blue, purple, scarlet and fine twined linen. These, as we shall see, speak to us of the official and personal glories of the Lord Jesus and, of course, in the sphere of God's habitation, in the sphere of the assembly, with the help and illumination of the Holy Spirit, these are made good to us, brought before us for our hearts' enlightenment. The world knows nothing about that. This is only known in the sphere where God dwells where there is illumination by the Spirit of God.

The Coverings
Exodus 26. 1-14, 36-37

Having entered through the gate and considered the brazen altar and the brazen laver we come next to the tabernacle structure proper, with its door of entrance. We have already considered the boards of wood of the tabernacle structure proper which were overlaid with gold with their two tenons and their two sockets of silver, and how they were held together by five bars. We now turn to think of the curtain, the coverings and the door of entrance.

The tabernacle structure was comprised of twenty boards of one and a half cubits wide. Each board was ten cubits high and the tabernacle was ten cubits broad. It was thus thirty cubits long by ten cubits high by ten cubits broad. One cubit is possibly twenty inches and was the measurement of a woman's arm (reckoned to be twenty inches on average) from elbow to fingertip. The idea of measurements being taken from the human body indicates that here is truth that is infinite brought down to finite understanding.

It is important to observe that it had two sets of curtains and two sets of coverings. There were curtains of fine twined linen, blue, purple, and scarlet and on top of them there were curtains of goats' hair. Over this there were the two coverings of rams' skins dyed red and the covering of the badgers' skins.

Another important matter to observe is the employment of the three words 'tabernacle', 'tent', and 'covering'. A distinction is made between the tabernacle and his tent. 'Then a cloud covered the tent of the congregation, and the glory of the Lord filled the tabernacle', Exod. 40. 34. The cloud, on the outside, covered the tent but the glory of the Lord, on the inside, filled the tabernacle. The curtains of fine twined linen with blue, purple, and scarlet colours, wrought with needlework and having the cherubim thereon are spoken of as 'the tabernacle'. This is a distinct Hebrew word. Then, there were the curtains of goats' hair. The word that is employed with regard to them is the word for 'tent', which is quite another word. Thus the tabernacle was the

33

beautiful curtains and the tent the curtains of goats' hair. Thus, 'the tabernacle' relates to what was inside; these are the beauties of the person of Christ. 'The tent' relates to what was outside, the goat's hair covering showing that He was impervious to what might come from the world against Him.

The third Hebrew word is the word for 'covering' and this is employed for the rams' skins dyed red and the badgers' skins. These three words help us to understand what we are now considering.

The curtains, Exod. 26. 1-6.

Their dimensions

According to verse 1, these were ten in number and it is emphasized that each was the same length and breadth. Their length was twenty-eight cubits and breadth was four cubits, 26. 2.

In verse 3, the ten curtains were divided into two sets of five. Five curtains were looped together by loops of blue, there being fifty loops on each curtain. Then, the other five curtains were similarly looped together by loops of blue. Then, these two sets of five curtains were coupled together by fifty taches, or hooks, of gold so that the ten curtains became one tabernacle. 'And it shall be one tabernacle', 26. 6. Thus, as one piece, the dimensions would be twenty-eight cubits broad and forty cubits long.

As to the length of the structure (which was thirty cubits) these curtains, covering the top from the door backwards, would fall ten cubits over the back. Then, as to its breadth (which was ten cubits), there would be an overhang of nine cubits on each side. Since the structure was ten cubits high, the curtains would be short of touching the earth.

These numerals must be understood. There were ten curtains and I suggest that in that they were divided into two sets of five they speak of human responsibility. We have already seen this in terms of human responsibility God-ward and man-ward. The ten commandments were divided into two. The first half was with regard to man's responsibility God-ward; the second half was with regard to man's responsibility to his fellow man. It speaks to us of our glorious Lord, the only one who discharged completely and without any flaw man's dual responsibility to God and man. He both glorified God and loved men.

Then, they were twenty-eight cubits long and this divides into four by seven. We can readily understand the significance of the number four. Four is always the universal number. Ezekiel chapter 37 verse 9 speaks of the 'four winds' and Isaiah chapter 11 verse 12 speaks of the 'four corners of the earth'. We have already seen that it occurs frequently in the tabernacle: the brazen altar was foursquare and had four horns and the golden altar was also foursquare. The number seven speaks of perfection. We shall see this especially in the golden lampstand. In regard to our Lord Jesus Christ the number four suggests that He is the Saviour of the world and is the One who is destined to reign universally.

Details of curtains

Firstly, there were curtains made of *fine twined linen*. This speaks of the holy, perfect, righteous manhood of our glorious Lord. In Revelation chapter 19 the fine linen is the righteous acts of the saints. The root meaning of 'linen' is white, or bright. This needs to be considered carefully in these days when our Lord's impeccability is being challenged. We consider One who was impeccably holy. This does not simply mean that our Saviour did not sin, or that He would not sin, but rather that He could not do so. Because of this, some question the reason for His temptation. We are to remember that God and the Holy Spirit can each be tempted. Our Lord said, 'Thou shalt not tempt the Lord thy God', Matt. 4. 7. The Holy Spirit can be tempted. 'How is it that ye have agreed together to tempt the Spirit of the Lord?' Acts 5. 9. If temptation involves the possibility of succumbing we must apply that to God and the Holy Spirit also. We would never think of doing that and neither should we do so in regard to the person of our Lord Jesus.

Let us cling tenaciously to our Saviour's impeccability. This does not mean simply that He 'did no sin' in terms of 1 Peter chapter 2 verse 22. The thought there is that in circumstances of maltreatment He did no fault. That is all that Peter is saying there. Our Lord's impeccability is found in 1 John chapter 3 verse 5 which states that, 'in him is no sin'. This is an absolute statement. There never was, nor ever could be, sin in Him and this is beautifully pictured in the white of the fine linen.

'My beloved is white and ruddy' are the words of the bride, S. of S. 5. 10. That speaks of the Saviour. We are told that David was ruddy, 1 Sam. 16. 6-17, but it is never said of David that he was white. Indeed, it could not be said of any man save our Lord. Adam was an innocent man when he was created but he nevertheless had a capacity to sin. However, our Lord was holy. 'That holy thing that shall be born of thee shall be called the Son of God', Luke 1. 35. Our Lord had a nature that was impervious to sin and a body that was impervious to disease. He bore our sins sacrificially without being tainted by them. He bore our sicknesses sympathetically without experiencing any of them. He is the only exception to the divine verdict, 'There is none righteous, no, not one', Rom. 3. 10. Thus, when on the cross and numbered with the transgressors, the centurion was heard to say, 'Certainly, this was a righteous man', Luke 23. 47. The thief also said, when our Lord was numbered with the transgressors, 'This man hath done nothing amiss', 23. 41, or, literally, 'This man hath not done one thing out of place'.

'God cannot be tempted with evil', Jas 1. 13, means that God is not versed in evil in respect of temptation. James points out that God never tempts a man with evil. There are three types of temptation. There is temptation from God, from the devil and from one's fallen nature. When God tempts He does it to produce the best. It has three things in view: to prove, to disprove or to improve. He either proves virtue or disproves it by showing its absence; or He improves what might be there. When the devil tempts it is to produce the worst. He always has in view to come between the soul and God, to undermine one's trust in God. Thus, the devil was permitted to tempt Job, to come between him and his God. Temptation from our own sinful nature is to produce lust and evil desires.

Adam was not tempted from his fallen nature or by God but by the devil. All that was involved in that temptation was to obey or disobey God. Our Lord Jesus Christ was never attacked by a fallen nature. He said, 'The prince of this world cometh, and hath nothing in me', John 14. 30. He was not tempted by God either for He did not need to be proved or improved. As with Adam, His temptation came from the devil. Let us remember, too, that those temptations were divinely initiated as He was led by the Holy Spirit into the wilderness to be tempted to prove His impeccability. These are very important matters.

There are two things said of both our Lord and the church. He is 'a lamb without spot or blemish', 1 Pet. 1. 18, and this is what He was inherently. Ephesians chapter 5 verse 27 says of the church that it is 'holy and without blemish' and it is this by divine grace. What was true of Him inherently became true of His people by reason of His work at Calvary.

'*Fine*' links with the fine flour of the meal offering. Every stitch was fine so that the mesh was fine and beautiful. Each stitch was equal indicating that here was one in whom there was no discrepancy in word and thought, one who was perfectly blended.

Blue is the heavenly colour. In Exodus chapter 24, Moses, Aaron, Nadab and Abihu, and seventy elders of Israel went up into the top of the mountain and saw the God of Israel. Under His feet was as it were a paved work of sapphire stone.

Let us think of our Lord Jesus Christ in His heavenly character. This is John's presentation of Christ. 'Ye are from beneath; I am

37

from above: ye are of this world; I am not of this world', John 8. 23. 'I am the living bread which came down from heaven', John 6. 51. To those who could appreciate it He brought down the very fragrance of heaven itself. Psalm 45 verse 8 says, 'All thy garments *smell* of myrrh, and aloes, *and* cassia'. What this must have meant in a dark, squalid world! Here was One who not only is white and heavenly (taking character from heaven) but who was out of heaven as one who gave character to heaven. 'The first man *is* of the earth, earthy: the second man *is* the Lord out of heaven', 1 Cor. 15. 47. Paul might have been expected to say that 'the second Man was out of heaven, heavenly' but he says He is 'the Lord out of heaven'. Adam was of the earth and took character from it, but our Lord is out of heaven, not as taking character from it but, in fact, giving character to it.

Purple is the imperial colour, the colour of Gentile royalty. In Judges chapter 8, there was purple raiment on the kings of Midian. In John's Gospel they clothed Him in a purple robe, described in Matthew as a scarlet robe. There were not two separate robes, as the timing of the events surrounding the narratives regarding the robe makes clear when the Gospels are compared. Evidently, what they put on our Lord was a Roman army officer's coat, which was scarlet, (and in its original state was gorgeous, Luke 23. 11) but it was not a new one and so looked more purple than scarlet. That is the literal explanation but there is a spiritual explanation. Purple points our attention not just to one who is king of the Jews but, as the imperial colour, points to one with universal dominion as the Son of Man, the one who is King of kings. 'Ask of me, and I shall give thee the heathen for thine inheritance, and the uttermost parts of the earth for thy possession' is the language of Psalm 2 verse 8. 'Thou madest him to have dominion over the works of thy hands; thou hast put all *things* under his feet', Ps. 8. 6. 'The kingdoms of this world are become *the kingdoms* of our Lord, and of his Christ; and he shall reign for ever and ever', Rev. 11. 15. These point our attention to the ruler of heaven and earth, the Lord of hosts of the Old Testament.

The scarlet speaks of Jewish royalty. In 2 Samuel chapter 1 verse 24 Saul clothed his daughters in scarlet. This colour speaks of the Lord Jesus Christ as the Son of David, great David's greater Son, who, in Luke chapter 1, is given the throne of his father David. The word for scarlet is 'worm scarlet', taken from a particular worm. No doubt the significance of this is that the one who is destined to sit on the throne of His father David had first of all to become a worm and not a man, Ps. 22. 6. It is the sufferings that lead to the throne. Thus, Matthew's Gospel, which speaks of the scarlet robe, starts rather significantly, 'The book of the generation of Jesus Christ, the son of David, the son of Abraham', Matt. 1. 1. As the Son of David, Solomon, He shall sit on the throne but as the son of Abraham, Isaac, He filled the altar.

John's Gospel is for the world. In it we read unique statements such as, 'He was in the world, and the world was made by him, and the world knew him not', John 1. 10, whereas in Matthew He was born king of the Jews. It is remarkable to observe that it was Gentile wise men who, at the beginning, said, 'Where is he that is born king of the Jews?' Matt. 2. 2, and it was a Gentile, Pilate, who at the end caused the superscription, 'This is Jesus the king of the Jews', Matt. 27. 37. What the Gentiles confessed the Jews denied. The scarlet robe was no doubt put on him in mockery but it will have its answer in wondrous reality in a day that is yet to be.

The *cherubim* are always connected with God's righteous character. In Genesis chapter 3, where they receive their first mention, there was placed on the east of the garden cherubim and a flaming sword. God would not permit man in his guilt to partake of the tree of life. Only when his sin was atoned for would man enjoy the gift of eternal life. Thus, between God and His holiness and man and his guilt, was the cherubim and the flaming sword. When we come to consider the mercy seat we shall again see the cherubim but no flaming sword. Instead of the flaming sword, we are gazing upon blood; the flaming sword is sheathed in a victim. The cherubim might therefore speak to us of one who came to meet the claims of the divine throne and who not only did that but will Himself yet judge the habitable earth in righteousness, Acts 17. 31, and hand back to God a purged and restored kingdom. Our Lord Jesus Christ is the only one able to do that.

The gate of the court has no cherubim, as entry through it was all of grace. A person entering by grace would then meet with the brazen altar, where the claims of divine righteousness were met. The gate was long and broad, indicating provision for all.

There were *two sets of five curtains* which were looped together by loops of blue. There were fifty loops in each curtain. These two sets of curtains, once they were looped together, were coupled together by fifty taches, or hooks, of gold. In this way the ten curtains became one tabernacle, one curtain. This seems to suggest that all the personal and official glories of Christ represented in these beautiful curtains were all fulfilled in one glorious person. It is all summed up in the Son of God who came from heaven; the gold taches speak of the Son of God and the blue loops remind us that He is the one who came from heaven.

Secondly, there were *the curtains of goats' hair,* vv. 7-13. These constituted the tent. Whereas there were ten curtains of fine twined linen, verse 7 indicates that there were eleven curtains of goats' hair. The curtains of fine twined linen were twenty-eight by four cubits, but the curtains of goats' hair were thirty by four cubits. Thus, there was one curtain more of goats' hair and each of these curtains was two cubits longer than the curtains of fine twined linen. These beautiful curtains of fine twined linen were therefore completely covered, v. 13.

The curtains of fine twined linen speak of what Christ was internally whilst the curtains of goats' hair speaks of what He is externally. Goats' hair is connected with His prophetic office, not so much as to His ministry but as to His separation from evil. In Zechariah chapter 13 verse 14, we read, 'The prophets shall be ashamed every one of his vision, when he hath prophesied; neither shall they wear a rough garment to deceive'. In John chapter 4, the woman of Samaria said to our Lord, after He said to her 'Thou hast no husband', 'I perceive that thou art a prophet'. She was convicted and the secrets of her heart were exposed but when she went to invite the men of Samaria she says, 'Come, see a man, which told me all things that ever I did: is not this the Christ?' The first part of that invitation is the goats' hair but the second part is the fine twined linen. She first saw Him in the goats' hair and then realized there was more to Him than she had first seen.

Verse 9 states that the sixth curtain was to be doubled. This is the same word as is used in regard to the high priest's garments, where doubling produced a pocket for the twelve stones which represented the tribes of Israel. Being doubled over the front of the tabernacle, it covered the hooks by which the door was suspended. That doubled curtain was to indicate the tent of meeting to which they gathered when God had something to say to them.

The covering of the tent, Exod. 26. 14.

The covering was firstly of *rams' skins dyed red*. There is no measurement given to this or the covering of badgers' skins. The ram is connected with consecration. At the time of the consecration of the priesthood, Exodus 29 and Leviticus 8, a ram was offered for the acceptance of the priests and for their sanctification. Its blood was sprinkled on their right ear, right thumb and the great toe of the right foot. The inwards and the right shoulder were put in the priest's hands and waved before the Lord. This was the priest's consecration.

The first mention of a ram was in Genesis chapter 22, where the ram was caught by the horns in a thicket. This ram, with no possibility of escape, speaks of one who had no desire to escape. He said, 'Lo I come to do thy will, O God', Heb. 10. 9. The Lord Jesus is seen as such in Luke chapter 2 verse 49, where He says, 'Wist ye not that I must be about my Father's business?' Again He says, 'Put up thy sword into the sheath: the cup which my Father hath given me, shall I not drink it?' John 18. 11. He was truly 'obedient unto death', Phil. 2. 8. In fact, in that the skins were dyed red we are reminded that His consecration was unto death. We sometimes sing H. L. ROSSIER's hymn,

> 'Lord, e'en to death Thy love could go,
> A death of shame and loss;
> To vanquish for us every foe,
> Thou dids't endure the cross'.

Secondly, there were coverings of *badgers' skins*. These were the external coverings. These must have been fastened together but when the tabernacle was in transit the badgers' skins also covered articles of furniture. The whole could not cover each one. In fact, the brazen altar was covered in purple and then badgers' skins were on top of that and in this we see that there was purple and badgers' skins distinct from what was in the beautiful curtains and the coverings.

In Ezekiel chapter 16, where we have the account of Israel's betrothal to God, He says 'Thus wast thou decked with gold and silver; and thy raiment was of fine linen, and silk, and broidered work', v. 13. There is not much beauty in badgers' skins, reminding us that 'he hath no form nor comeliness; and when we shall see him, there is no beauty that we should desire him', Isa. 53. 2. There was nothing about the Lord Jesus Christ to attract the human heart. He did not do things merely to cause His fellow men to esteem Him. What beauty there was in Him was internal and moral, such as His purity, grace, holiness, and insistence upon truth.

Keeping to the thought that this is the habitation of God by the Spirit, we might remember that, as they travelled, they saw nothing of the beautiful curtains or the goats' hair. All they saw was this badgers' skin covering. We ought to remember also that there is nothing about a New Testament assembly that appeals to the man of the world or to the flesh in the child of God. The assembly is to be a spiritual place. 'And of the rest durst no man join himself to them: but the people magnified them', Acts 5. 13.

The door

This led into the holy place through which the priests would enter to attend to their duties there.

The gate into the court was wide and low and had four pillars which perhaps refer to the four evangelists in their universal call, asking all to hear the Saviour say, 'Come unto me', Matt. 11. 28, but the door of the tabernacle was different in that it was narrow and high. This refers not to the call of grace but the call of the priests to priestly service.

The door was suspended by hooks of gold and supported by five pillars of shittim wood overlaid with gold, having sockets of copper. The door itself was of blue, purple, scarlet, and fine twined linen. The five pillars might refer to the five writers of the New Testament, just as the four pillars of the gate might refer to the four evangelists. Their teaching was higher and narrower. Their teaching concerning the Lord Jesus Christ was not as opening up the brazen altar, as something that is available to all, but regarding entry into the sanctuary for priestly sacrifice. Many go in at the gate and avail themselves of the altar but the door into the holy place distinguishes the common people from the priestly family. Thus it is today. Many are prepared to go in at the gate and avail themselves of the altar who do not go in at the narrow high door. They stop at that. In Acts chapter 18 all Asia heard the gospel, but in 2 Timothy chapter 1 all Asia was not prepared to follow Paul.

The door was suspended on hooks of gold. If the pillars speak of five writers of the epistles, then the hooks of gold speak of the divine inspiration of the epistles. There is a need to remember that the epistles are as inspired as the Gospels and that it would be wrong to suggest, as some do, that Paul's writings were, somehow, not as inspired as were the evangelists.

Having entered through the door everything was pure. Pure gold met the gaze: the pure gold of the lampstand, the pure lamp, pure oil, pure table and pure frankincense. All are described as pure and so entering into the tabernacle one was confronted with pure things. It is little wonder that the ministry of the laver was first needed.

The Court and the hangings of the court
(Exodus 27. 9-19)

The hangings of the court formed the perimeter of the tabernacle and these, therefore, are what would confront the one who approached.

There were *sixty pillars* in all. There were twenty on the south and north sides, ten on the west side and ten on the east side. On the east side there were three pillars on each side of the gate, while another four pillars, the pillars of the gate, were viewed apart. There were sixty valiant men who guarded Solomon's bed, S. of S. 3. 7. Sixty speaks of the believer in valiant, unblemished testimony in the wilderness of this world.

The *height* of the pillars is not specified. It is often said they were five cubits high and that would be true up to a point because the hangings, which were hung upon the pillars, were themselves five cubits high.

There is no mention of the *material* from which the pillars were made. Chapter 27 verse 10 says, 'And the twenty pillars thereof and their twenty sockets *shall be of* brass; the hooks of the pillars and their fillets *shall be of* silver'. Because of this verse some have taught that the pillars were made of brass but, when the italicised words are omitted, the verse reads, 'and the twenty pillars thereof and their twenty sockets, brass'. Thus, the sockets were of brass but not the pillars. This is an important omission. It has been accepted by many that they were made of shittim wood, which might be so, but that is not actually stated. The material from which the boards of the tabernacle structure were made is clearly stated to be shittim wood and gold; this speaks of the believer's standing in the presence of God, an habitation of God through the Spirit. In the court, however, it is not so much a picture of an habitation of God by the Spirit but the believer in his testimony man-ward. Upon the pillars was hanging the fine twined linen, which the outsider would see first of all.

45

Because the pillars speak of testimony man-ward there should be no surprise that there is no mention made of the material from which they were made. After all, when it comes to testimony it must always be, 'Not I but Christ'. In this world the believer is associated with the testimony not that he might be seen but that Christ might be seen. In the divine presence the believer is seen in all the acceptability of the work of Christ, but when it comes to testimony to the world it must always be 'Not I but Christ'. The emphasis is not what they were made of but the purpose they served; that upon them hangs that which speaks of the person and character of our Lord Jesus Christ.

Verse 10 speaks of the *sockets* of the pillars. Each had a socket made of brass, or copper, 27. 10. That verse also speaks of their *fillets*, or connecting rods, which were made of silver, and so these sixty pillars stood up on sockets of brass and were connected by fillets of silver running right round the perimeter. Chapter 38 also speaks of chapiters, or ornamental crowns, of silver on top of each pillar. 'And the sockets for the pillars *were of* brass; the hooks of the pillars and their fillets *of* silver; and the overlaying of their chapiters *of* silver'.

It is no surprise that the brazen altar was made of copper because it is the greatest heat resisting metal, and the fire was always burning in it. The foundation of these pillars was made of the same metal that resisted the fire upon the altar. This indicates that believers have a standing upon the great truth, that a just God has justified him that believeth in Jesus. When the apostle Paul says in Romans chapter 3 verse 26, 'that he might be just, and the justifier of him which believeth in Jesus', he is not saying that God is just when He now justifies us but that it is a just God who has dealt righteously with the question of our sins at Calvary. He is the one who now justifies the man or woman who believes in Jesus. This is what we have here; we rest on the truth that it is a just God who has dealt in righteousness with our sin and guilt at Calvary and it is He who justifies us. The fire has exhausted itself in the copper and on that ground we have a standing in His presence; we are justified by a just God.

The hooks were made of silver, 27. 10. The purpose of the hooks was to have hung upon them the fine twined linen. Silver speaks of the redemptive work of Christ. We can only represent Christ to the world in virtue of what Christ has done for us; we could have never done this naturally. This is the main product of the redemptive work of Christ as far as the world is concerned, the presentation of the person of Christ.

The *chapiters* were ornamental crowns on top of each pillar, made of silver. This silver speaks of the hope of redemption. Our redemption is not yet complete; there is a hope connected to it. This crown of redemption is found in Romans chapter 8 verse 23. 'We ourselves groan within ourselves, waiting for the adoption, *to wit,* the redemption of our body'. These pillars are out in the wilderness; we do not know the material of which they were made but the crown, the hope of redemption, reminds us of redemption not yet accomplished for which we wait and hope, namely the redemption of the body when our Lord shall come. These bodies of our humiliation shall be changed and fashioned like to His body of glory. Our bodies still belong to a groaning creation but when our bodies are redeemed the hope of redemption will be fully realized.

Each pillar also had *pins and cords.* 'The pins of the tabernacle, and the pins of the court, and their cords', 35. 18. Cords were attached to each pillar and these cords were held safely to the ground by a pin, almost like a tent peg. These pins and cords gave the pillar security against the winds, storms and tempest of the wilderness. The pins and the cords have to do with keeping power that will keep us as long as we are here. We may praise God that while He has saved us with an eternally secure salvation He has also given us that which will give us security against the wind and the tempest, the trials of the wilderness journey. Peter says that we are 'kept by the power of God through faith unto salvation ready to be revealed in the last time', 1 Pet. 1. 5.

The *fillets of silver* were connecting rods which joined all the pillars together and thus connected them. The silver speaks again of the redemptive work of Christ. It is that work which connects the saints together in their testimony. The work of Christ has brought together people who might otherwise have never known each other, from different backgrounds and different walks of life, in testimony to Himself.

There were *hangings of fine twined* linen hanging on these sixty pillars. We learn that there were 280 cubits of fine twined linen; on the south and north sides there were 100 cubits, on the west side fifty cubits and on the east side there were fifteen cubits on each side of the gate, leaving twenty cubits for the gate itself. The height of the fine twined linen was five cubits. Accordingly, the fine twined linen measured 280 by 5 cubits.

This speaks of the real humanity of our Saviour. Two hundred and eighty days is the period of gestation from conception to birth, reminding us of one who was here as a real man and who lived a life of practical, consistent righteousness. We cannot emphasize enough the perfect, real, though unique, humanity of our Lord Jesus Christ.

The fine twined linen speaks of Christ. Anyone who approached the tabernacle was met by an unbroken wall of white. Here, the assembly is pictured in its testimony man-ward, presenting Christ in all His purity and in His practical righteousness. This is the teaching of 2 Corinthians chapter 3 verse 3 which says, *'Forasmuch as ye are* manifestly declared to be the epistle of Christ ministered by us, written not with ink, but with the Spirit of the living God'. As people of the locality see the assembly in its testimony man-ward they should see an unbroken wall of white, a presentation of Jesus as He was when He was here. It is possible that because of his conduct a believer could be a blemish on that otherwise unbroken wall of white. These are important but practical matters.

'But ye have not so learned Christ; if so be that ye have heard him, and have been taught by him, as the truth is in Jesus' is the remarkable language of Ephesians chapter 5 verses 20-21. When it is a practical matter of what affects our testimony it is a question of the truth not as it is in Christ but as it is in Jesus. The reason for this is that Jesus is the standard for our practical Christian living. John says, 'He that saith he abideth in him ought himself also so to walk, even as he walked', 1 John 2. 6. Peter says, 'Christ also suffered for us, leaving us an example, that ye should follow his steps', 1 Pet. 2. 21. Paul says, 'Be ye followers of me, even as I also *am* of Christ', 1 Cor. 11. 1. This is the presentation to the world of the practical righteousness of Christ Himself in the world which gave Him a cross and rejected Him.

There are various words for linen. Later on in Exodus there are the linen breeches of the priests. They were made of rough, or flaxen, linen but here it is fine twined linen as it speaks of Christ. It is like the fine flour of the meal offering. It is linen that is beautiful and even, fine in its texture, without flaw, perfect in every detail, reminding us of the One who was righteous in every way.

The Brazen Altar
Exodus 27. 1-5

In the Old Testament the brazen altar is given a threefold designation. It is called simply 'the altar', 27. 1; 28. 43; 29. 12; 30. 20 and in many other places, 'the altar of burnt offering', 30. 28 and nine other times, 'the table of the Lord', Mal. 1. 7, 12.

There were two altars in the tabernacle. An altar made of copper was in the court and another, made of gold, in the holy place. The copper, or brazen, altar is called 'the altar' in that it was basic to all that pertained to the tabernacle ritual. It was the most used of all the vessels of the tabernacle. On it there were offered the morning and evening sacrifices, the daily sacrifices, the yearly sacrifice of the Day of Atonement and many more beside. Moreover, that same hallowed fire that burned on that brazen altar was taken in and burned upon the golden altar and, on the Day of Atonement, the same fire from the brazen altar was carried in by the high priest in the live coals on the golden censer. The brazen altar is thus connected with the holy place and the holiest of all.

In Leviticus chapter 4, in connection with the sin offering, it is repeatedly spoken of as 'the altar of burnt offering'. This particularly brings before us the altar in its God-ward aspect; the ascending offering was that which all ascended to God as a sweet savour. When Malachi speaks twice of the altar as 'the table of the Lord' however, he refers to its man-ward aspect, in connection with divine provision.

Its position

'And thou shalt set the altar of the burnt offering before the door of the tabernacle of the tent of the congregation', Exod. 40. 6. In fact, it was placed just inside the gate, though this verse does not tell us this. The significance of its position as described in this verse is that it was the basis of approach to God and the ground of meeting with Him. It stood just within the gate which was at the perimeter of the tabernacle and was the first thing to be seen on entering the court.

God dwelt between the cherubim on the mercy seat on the west of the tabernacle. The gate was on the east side. The first thing to be illuminated by the rising sun was the beautiful gate. The lovely hangings of the court presented an unbroken wall of white; that wall of white was broken as to its colour by the gate of the court. That gate was twenty cubits broad, five cubits high and was made of blue, purple, scarlet, and fine twined linen. The light of the sun falling on these colours must have presented a beautiful sight. The gate of four colours was suspended upon four pillars. This is suggestive of the four evangelists who have one voice in testimony to Christ as the way, the truth and the life, apart from whom no one could come to the Father, John 14. 6. I would suggest that this is the prime significance of the gate. These four evangelists seem to direct out attention to the words of our Saviour, 'Come unto me, all ye that labour and are heavy laden, and I will give you rest', Matt. 11. 28.

The unique person represented in these colours is presented in the four Gospels.

John tells us what is represented by the blue as he speaks of the Son of God, the one who is heavenly in His character. In John He says, 'Ye are from beneath; I am from above: ye are of this world; I am not of this world', 8. 23, and 'I came forth from the Father, and am come into the world: again, I leave the world, and go to the Father', 16. 28.

Luke tells us what is represented in the purple. This is the colour of Gentile royalty. Luke tells us that He is the Son of Man; He is not just the son of David (which is limited in its scope) but as the Son of Man there is committed to Him universal dominion. Accordingly Luke traces His genealogy back to Adam; the whole race is involved in the incoming of God's Son into the world.

Matthew tells us what is represented in the scarlet, the colour of Jewish royalty. He is the son of David, and so in Matthew His genealogy is traced back to David and Abraham, not Adam. Matthew commences with the one who was 'born king of the Jews', 2. 2, and He is, in that Gospel, great David's greater Son.

Mark tells us about the fine twined linen. It speaks not of what He is officially but of the one who was the perfect servant, lovely, pure and holy. If we think of Him as the one who was 'finely twined', we remember one who never needed to be chastised or His spirit refined. He was never ill humoured.

Thus, we hear Him say, 'I am the way, the truth, and the life: no man cometh unto the Father, but by me', John 14. 6. As we enter the gate of the tabernacle and see the altar we may learn that, though glorious in Himself, sacrifice was necessary; to bring us to God blood must be shed. This is what is encountered at the brazen altar.

Its dimensions

The brazen altar was the biggest item of tabernacle furniture and was exactly twice the size of the ark.

The altar was *five cubits long*, five cubits broad and three cubits high, 27. 1. The numerals are significant. 'Five' is the number of human responsibility. A man or woman normally has five toes and five fingers, with which to discharge their responsibility, and five senses. In Daniel chapter 2, in connection with Nebuchadnezzar's image which speaks of government entrusted to the hand of man, mention is made of five materials. Gold, silver, brass, iron and clay all speak of human responsibility.

This all signifies that the altar entirely met the claims of God on responsible man. 'The soul that sinneth, it shall die', Ezek. 18. 20. This was true of all men; we praise God for an altar that has met the claims of God upon sinful, responsible man.

It was therefore foursquare, 27. 1, and the repetition of the number 'four' is to be noted. In that it was foursquare, we learn that at Calvary, no matter how we view it, there was no diminution in the judgement He endured. There is also the suggestion that the cross equally meets the need of all mankind, whether to the north, south, east or west.

The altar was also *three cubits high.* This might speak of the three-fold testimony to man's sin. The superscription on the cross was written in three languages. Hebrew was the language of the religious world; Latin speaks of the power of this world and Greek of its wisdom. The three-fold guilt of the world was written over the cross. That three-fold testimony to man's sin gives testimony to the fact that man's complete need has been met.

Some think that three will speak of the involvement of the Godhead in the death of Christ: 'How much more shall the blood of Christ, who through the eternal Spirit offered himself without spot to God, purge your conscience from dead works to serve the living God', Heb. 9. 14.

Three is also the number of resurrection. Thus, even as we think of the altar that speaks of His death, we are glad to know that death was not the end of everything. 'Thou wilt not leave my soul in hell', Ps. 16. 10. In Psalm 22 the Lord Jesus is 'the hind of the morning'. 'Weeping may endure for a night, but joy cometh in the morning', Ps. 30. 5.

Its design

There was a *horn* upon each of the four corners, Exod. 27. 2. When animals were brought to the altar they were bound to these horns, Ps. 118. 27. These beasts came unwillingly and ignorantly to the place of sacrifice, unlike our Lord. 'Jesus therefore, knowing all things that should come upon him, went forth', John 18. 4. Old Testament sacrifices could not escape; our Lord had no desire to do so. He said, 'Lo, I come to do thy will, O God' and it is by this will that 'we are sanctified through the offering of the body of Jesus Christ', Heb. 10. 9, 10. In Solomon's day both Adonijah 1 Kgs. 1. 50, and Joab, 1 Kgs. 2. 28, caught hold of the horns of the altar. Adonijah was saved but Joab was slain. Adonijah speaks of saving faith whereas Joab was an apostate. Apostasy is a sin for which there is no forgiveness. 'The sin of Judah is written with a pen of iron, and with the point of a diamond: it is graven upon the table of their heart, and upon the horns of your altars', Jer. 17. 1.

The horn always speaks of strength or power. While it was used in the first instance that the animal might be bound securely to the powerful horn so that it would not escape, there are other thoughts connected with the horns as symbolizing power. They might speak to us of the language of the Lord when He said concerning His life, 'I have power to lay it down, and I have power to take it again', John 10. 18. The fact that there are four horns speaks of His power to meet a universal need.

The altar was made 'hollow with boards', Exod. 27. 8. The altar was thus *a hollow, square box* and the sacrifice was placed inside it. This might link up our thoughts with the one who, in Philippians chapter 2, 'made himself of no reputation', or 'emptied himself'; He did not, of course, empty Himself of deity but in self-humiliation in coming down to where we were. Elsewhere, on the eve of Calvary, He speaks to the Father of 'the glory which I had with thee before the world was', John 17. 5. The extent of His emptying is seen in that 'though he was rich, yet for your sakes he became poor, that ye through his poverty might be rich', 2 Cor. 8. 9.

Then, chapter 27 verses 4-5 speak of its *grate* of network with four brazen rings in its corners. Somehow these rings protruded through the angle of the altar and through these rings were put the staves upon which the altar was carried during the travels of the children of Israel. This network of grate was in the midst of the altar and it not only made the whole altar secure by reason of the rings being put through the angles but it was the means by which the whole thing was supported when it was carried by the

Kohathites. The ashes were removed by shovels and it is likely that there was a space at the bottom of the altar to assist their removal.

In the tabernacle there were three things the same height. These were the grate in the midst of the altar, the mercy seat and the table of shewbread. This indicates that the sacrifice meets the claims of the throne of God, at the mercy seat, and provides the basis of fellowship between God and men, the table of shewbread.

The sacrifice and the fire were burning in the midst of the altar. The Israelite who brought His offering witnessed it being killed and placed on the altar but it was really only the eye of God that saw what was going on in the midst of the altar. In this connection we may think of the Lord's inward, internal sufferings. There were two sides to our Lord's sufferings. He had a cup to drink, which He would take internally and a baptism to be baptized with, which was external. It was His inward sufferings on the tree which were atoning. 'Thou shalt make his soul an offering for sin', Isa. 53. 10. He suffered in the darkness but these were not His only internal sufferings; the darkness merely shut out man's eye. In the garden of Gethsemane He said, 'My soul is exceeding sorrowful, even unto death', Matt. 26. 38, but His experience in the garden internally was anticipative of the experience that was soon to be realized on the cross. Only the suffering upon the cross was vicarious. What our Saviour suffered at the hands of men only condemned man; what meets our need is His internal sufferings on the tree. Nothing, therefore, that man inflicted upon Him could procure our salvation.

Distinction is made in Hebrews chapter 2 verses 9-10 between the 'suffering' of death and the 'sufferings' which He endured in His offices as the captain of our salvation and high priest. His sufferings from the manger to the cross were connected with His priesthood but His suffering on the tree is connected with His Saviour-hood. At man's hand He was oppressed and afflicted and led like a lamb to the slaughter 'yet He opened not His mouth',

Isa. 53. 7; but during the hours of darkness He cried, 'My God, my God, why hast thou forsaken me? why art thou so far from helping me, and from the words of my roaring?' Ps. 22. 1. The wounding and the bruising that He endured, Isa. 53. 5, were from God. This answers to Zechariah chapter 13 verse 7, 'Awake, O sword, against my shepherd, and against the man that is my fellow, saith the Lord of hosts'. 'It pleased the Lord to bruise him', Isa. 53. 10. He knew the chastening hand of God that we might know peace and by His stripe, from that same hand, we are healed.

Its materials

The brazen altar was made of two materials. 'Thou shalt make an altar of shittim wood . . . and thou shalt overlay it with brass', Exod. 27. 1, 2. Brass here is really copper. Copper is a metal which is noted for its fire resistant property and this is the main thought in the copper.

Seasoning of timber would normally take a period of up to four years but the acacia wood was suited to the tabernacle as it grew in the wilderness and was devoid of much of the sap in ordinary trees. It could be used almost as soon as it was cut down and this was especially useful as the tabernacle was constructed so soon after leaving Egypt. Additionally, wood was not exposed to the elements in the brazen altar as it was all overlaid with brass. It is possible that the only exposed acacia wood was found in the pillars of the court but it is not specifically stated that they were made of wood.

The *acacia wood* speaks of our Lord's humanity. It grew in the wilderness and was the only one of the materials of the tabernacle that was not brought from Egypt. It reminds us, when we think of our Lord Jesus Christ, that He was 'as a root out of a dry ground', Isa. 53. 10. In connection with the wooden boards of the tabernacle, we have seen that the wood speaks of our humanity and the fact that we have a standing in the presence of God, resting on the foundation of redemption and clothed in divine

57

righteousness. Thus, the acacia wood speaks of humanity in a general way.

The picture is not that the acacia wood had to be cut down, because the wood for the boards also had to be cut down, but that His manhood was necessary to His sacrifice. He was truly the seed of the woman. Almost every reference to His incarnation refers to the fact that He came to die, cp. Rom. 8. 3, and Gal. 4. 4. Our Lord was made a little lower than the angels with a view to the suffering of death. Accordingly, in the wood it is not so much the idea of seeing the glory of the Word made flesh in His holy, lovely, spotless humanity but the person of Christ in connection with the fires of Calvary and His capability of going into death. The force of Hebrews chapter 2 verse 14 is that He voluntarily took part in something that was outside of Himself; 'forasmuch then as the children are partakers of flesh and blood, he also himself likewise took part of the same'. Here was the only one capable of taking our place in death, one whose manhood was perfect but unique.

The acacia wood was expertly overlaid to the exclusion of all air so that it was never charred or burnt despite excessive heat. Though He was a man, He was not subject to death or liable to judgement. Because of His sinlessness He was neither a mortal man nor a sinful man; therefore, death had no claim upon Him and justice could make no demands.

Copper, with its ability to resist heat, speaks of righteousness. It was because of our Lord's righteous character that He was able to sustain and exhaust the fire of God's wrath. In fact, in the tabernacle gold, fine twined linen and copper all speak of righteousness. In gold there is divine righteousness and in fine twined linen there is seen our Lord's practical righteousness as He lived here as a man. In copper there is seen not so much His righteousness in relation to God but to the world; not so much God's character as His righteous dealing with evil.

There was only one who was able to sustain and exhaust in finite time the fire of God's wrath against sin. In eternity it will never exhaust itself on the impenitent but in finite time it exhausted itself at the place called Calvary. This should bow the heart of the believer, who shall never estimate or understand what our Saviour endured. Every other man who goes under God's wrath will never come out of it, as 'the wrath of God *abideth* on him', John 3. 36, but the Lord Jesus went under it and also came out of it. There were no ashes at Calvary for there the fire did not exhaust the sacrifice; rather, the sacrifice exhausted the fire.

In the case of the golden candlestick the oil kept the fire burning but at the altar a fire came out from before the Lord, Lev. 9. 24. This was hallowed fire. Nadab and Abihu offered strange fire in Leviticus chapter 10 and, as a result, came under divine judgement, whereas at Carmel it was fire from heaven that burned Elijah's sacrifice; this, therefore, was hallowed fire. It is interesting to observe also that both at the setting up of the tabernacle and at Pentecost God sent down fire from heaven to give testimony to Himself.

The fire at the altar was slow burning but outside the camp, where the sin offering was burnt, it was a devouring flame that speedily reduced the sacrifice to ashes.

There is one further matter regarding the materials of the altar. In Numbers chapter 16, the rebellion of Korah and others against the priesthood is recounted. It resulted in their death in remarkable circumstances and in their brazen censers being taken. From them they made broad plates for a covering of the sides of the altar. Thus, every time they approached the altar after this incident there was a witness to them that there was only one priesthood ordained by God and that God's judgement would fall on those who would usurp it.

The Brazen Altar

Its accessories

There were vessels that were employed in connection with the use of the altar, Exod. 27. 3. We must try and learn as to what use these five vessels were put to help us understand what took place at the brazen altar.

There were *pans* to receive the ashes and any residual fat so that the altar might be cleansed. In Numbers chapter 4 the ashes, when they were removed from the altar before it was moved through the wilderness, had to be treated in the manner directed by God. They were to be taken from the altar by a priestly man dressed in linen garments and placed by the east side of the altar. Then, he would put on other garments and 'carry forth the ashes without the camp unto a clean place', Lev. 6. 11. This is symbolic of our Lord's burial by Joseph, a rich and righteous man, in a clean place, the new tomb. He had been taken by wicked hands and crucified and slain, but the clean hands of Joseph had buried Him. The ashes were precious to God in terms of what they signified. The *shovels* were used to remove the ashes.

Basins were used to catch the blood. The horns of the altar were anointed by the blood of the sin offering for the ruler and the common people, and the rest was poured out at the bottom of the altar. If the sin offering was for the congregation or the anointed priest the blood was sprinkled on the horns of the golden altar and before the vail; the rest was poured out at the base of the altar. On the Day of Atonement blood was sprinkled on the golden altar and on and before the mercy seat.

Fire pans were used to carry the fire during the journey in the wilderness. The fire was hallowed and was never to be put out by wilful and positive act, or go out because of neglect.

The *flesh hooks* were used to turn the sacrifice so that it was completely roasted and so that its parts could be put in their respective places as they were put in order on the altar. God delights in order in worship and judged the sons of Eli who, in a later day, used these flesh hooks to satisfy their own lusts.

Its rings and staves

The staves, Exod. 27. 6-7, were employed for the journeying of the children of Israel that this amazing vessel might be carried. Paul might have this in mind when he speaks of 'always bearing about in the body the dying of the Lord Jesus, that the life also of Jesus might be made manifest in our body', 2 Cor. 4. 10, and 'the preaching of the cross', 1 Cor. 1. 18. No matter where they were, in the camp or on the journey, the brazen altar was with them; they were never far away from the altar. It is good to remember the words of the hymn, 'Jesus, keep me near the cross'.

There was put over it a purple cloth, Num. 4. 13, and on top a covering of badgers' skins. All that could be seen was the rough badgers' skin. There was nothing attractive about those badgers' skins but underneath was the purple cloth that speaks of dignity and royalty. The purple cloth represents what we understand of the cross but the badgers' skins of what the world thinks of it, for the preaching of the cross is foolishness to them.

In Hebrews chapter 13 the altar relates to us, 'We have an altar'. That altar is nothing visible or tangible but it is Calvary in remembrance, a sacrifice made once and for all that requires no repetition. There was daily attendance at the brazen altar, a constant vigil, and smoke always ascending; sacrifices were continually being made and blood was continually flowing. How different it is now! We have an altar; Calvary continually in remembrance, a sacrifice made once and for all. In fact, Christ is everything. He is the priest, the sacrifice, the offerer, and the altar.

The Brazen Laver and its Foot
Exodus 30. 17-21; 38. 8

The laver is interesting from the standpoint that we are given no dimensions and no reference is made to its design. There are no references to staves to transport it or anything to cover it; there are so many omissions.

The laver itself was the receptacle, or a kind of reservoir, that contained the water which the priests used to wash their hands and feet when they served in the tabernacle. Some think the laver itself was for washing the hands and the foot for washing the feet but it seems inconceivable that the priests would continually wash both hands and feet in the same water. Their hands were continually dealing with the blood of the sacrifices and their feet were continually treading the desert.

I suggest that the laver was the large receptacle and between the laver and its foot, there was a stem. A pipe ran through this stem and, perhaps by means of a tap, water would be supplied to the foot as it was required. There at the foot fresh water would be supplied each time for the washing of both the hands and feet of the priests.

'Thou shalt also make a laver of brass, and his foot also of brass, to wash withal', Exod. 30. 18. The King James Version places the word 'withal' in italics. The same language is used in Exodus chapter 40 verse 30. In chapter 30 verse 19 the King James Version says, 'Aaron and his sons shall wash their hands and their feet thereat', but *The Newberry Bible* renders it 'therefrom' and 'from it'. The word 'therein' is never used. The laver was the receptacle, therefore, and water somehow was filled into the foot and was available as they continually washed their hands and feet.

Its position

We are left in no doubt about this. 'Thou shalt put it between the tabernacle of the congregation and the altar', Exod. 30. 18.

Therefore, the laver was the second vessel, after the altar, that the priest would encounter on entering the gate into the court.

There is a two-fold thought. At the brazen altar we have the blood; at the brazen laver we have the water. At the brazen altar the blood was shed; it was sprinkled upon the horns of that altar and poured out at its base but at the brazen laver there is water for washing hands and feet. Repeatedly in scripture, blood and water are mentioned together. They are linked at the consecration of priests when Moses first of all washed each of the priests all over, Deut. 8 and Exod. 29, and, having done this, he clothed them. Also, he sprinkled blood upon their right ears, their right thumbs and the big toe of their right feet and so at the consecration of the priests water and blood were employed.

The same is true regarding the cleansing of the leper. The leper was cleansed all over and his hands sprinkled with the blood seven times.

In the New Testament we read, 'one of the soldiers with a spear pierced his side, and forthwith came there out blood and water', John 19. 34. Sometimes it is explained that this indicates that He died of a broken heart, but that is not the explanation. In fact there is no physical or medical explanation of this remarkable event. This was a matter that was divine and it signifies the meeting of our complete need. 'This is he that came by water and blood, even Jesus Christ; not by water only, but by water and blood', 1 John 5. 6.

This general truth is brought before us quite frequently in the New Testament. In 1 Corinthians chapter 6 verse 11, we read that 'such were some of you: but ye are washed' by water, 'but ye are sanctified, but ye are justified', by blood. In Hebrews chapter 10 verse 22, we read, 'Let us draw near with a true heart in full assurance of faith, having our hearts sprinkled (by blood) from an evil conscience, and our bodies washed with pure water'.

We require the action of both the blood and the water. Blood was necessary because of our guilt; water because of our natural state. Blood is connected with judicial cleansing from the guilt of sin; water is connected with the fact of our new birth, our regeneration. Thus, our need was two-fold: we required not only the question of our sins to be dealt with by blood, but we were by nature dead and required the water. Accordingly, those who are regenerate are those who are 'born of water and of the Spirit', John 3. 5. It is interesting to observe that in John chapter 3 the Holy Spirit is connected with the water and not the blood. This is because that chapter is dealing not so much with the forgiveness of sins and the removal of guilt but the new birth, which is connected with water and the Spirit. 'Water' speaks of the word and 'spirit' is the Holy Spirit. This links with 1 Peter chapter 1 verse 23, 'Being born again, not of corruptible seed, but of incorruptible, by the word of God, which liveth and abideth for ever'. It is so important to see things in their context.

Set in the court of the tabernacle, the laver was associated particularly with the priests. They were the only ones who washed at it and it was therefore not really connected with the ordinary Israelite. We have considered blood and water in a general sense but here was something rather different from that. The laver is not presented to us so much as meeting the sinner's need but in terms of what was requisite for priestly service and priestly approach to God.

This should cause heart searching before God. The altar and the laver go together. Some are happy about altar truth but are unconcerned regarding laver truth. In other words, some are quite content to be positionally correct, but are little concerned about being conditionally correct. But both are brought together in the scriptures. It is one thing to quote, 'Come out from among them, and be ye separate', 2 Cor. 6. 17, but the apostle goes on to say, 'Having therefore these promises, dearly beloved, let us cleanse ourselves from all filthiness of the flesh and spirit, perfecting holiness in the fear of God', 2 Cor. 7. 1. It is not enough to come out and be separate; we need to perfect holiness in the fear of God.

Its use

A two-fold use is specified. First, when going into the holy place, the tent of meeting, to attend the golden altar, the lampstand or the table of showbread, the priests were to wash with water 'that they die not'. Second, when they came near to the altar to offer or sacrifice they had to wash with water. There is, then, a link between the court and the holy place. To handle holy things one must be clean. Feet that would tread the holy place must be washed as must hands that would burn incense and attend the golden lampstand and the table of shewbread. This is an important matter. Though the use of the laver was exclusive to the priestly family, its truth may be applied to believers today because we are both offerer and priests. As offerers, we bring our offering and in a priestly way we present it as a holy priesthood.

Solemn attention needed to be given to this matter of cleansing. The necessity for priestly washing is emphasized by the repetition of the expression 'that they die not', Exod. 30. 20-21, and by the fact that verse 21 says, 'It shall be a statute for ever to them, even to him and to his seed throughout their generations'. The Holy Spirit bears ample testimony to this important but practical truth that to handle holy things one must be clean. 'Who shall ascend into the hill of the Lord? or who shall stand in his holy place? He that hath clean hands, and a pure heart', Ps. 24. 3-4. 'Follow peace with all men, and holiness, without which no man shall see the Lord', Heb. 12. 14. 'I will therefore that men pray every where, lifting up holy hands', 1 Tim. 2. 8. This is the truth of the laver and it is an exceedingly practical matter.

In John chapter 13 verse 10, our Lord employed two different words when He indicated that the person who is 'bathed' all over needs not save to 'wash' his feet. Bathing all over refers to the once for all consecration of the priesthood but washing the feet refers to the daily washing of feet at the laver. The priests were initially washed all over by Moses but, at the laver, they washed their own hands and feet. All over washing signifies new birth; it is never to be repeated. Thereafter, feet washing is necessary and must be repeated because of daily defilement. This is not so much washing from positive sin but the washing away of everything that is unworthy of God and unsuited to His presence. Those who handle holy things must be clean. In John chapter 13 the order is most beautiful. It commences with John's feet in Jesus' hands and ends with John's head on Jesus' bosom. The order is, therefore, cleansing before communion; there can be no communion apart from cleansing. Our Saviour said, 'If I wash thee not thou hast no part with me', not, 'no part in me'. Thus, the Lord Jesus Christ made it clear that communion without cleansing is impossible.

The idea in Numbers chapter 19, in connection with the provision for cleansing by the ashes of the red heifer, is that of being unwillingly defiled by the way in the wilderness journey. There is no thought of positive sin in that chapter but there were many ways in which one could be defiled. Where this occurred, the defiled person had to be washed in water in connection with the ashes of the red heifer. The ashes were a testimony to a sacrifice that had been made and washing in them was available on the journey when a sacrifice could not be made. The washing resulted in cleansing. This is John chapter 13; it is not positive sin but defilement by those things we encounter day by day in our daily life in a wicked world which, despite ourselves, defiles us. The water makes good to us the value of Calvary.

We learn in all of this that it is not enough to be assured or satisfied that one is judicially right with God in that the guilt of my sins has been dealt with (which is the truth of the brazen altar) but all daily defilement must also be washed away. 'Be ye clean, that bear the vessels of the Lord', Isa. 52. 11, is an imperative which is good for all time.

Accordingly, what is brought before us in the laver is, 'Be ye holy; for I am holy', 1 Pet. 1. 16.

Its material

'Thou shalt also make a laver of brass, and his foot also of brass', Exod. 30. 18. The brazen altar was made of wood and copper but the laver only of copper. The laver made of copper emphasizes not the person of Christ but His character, the righteous One who is the propitiation for our sins. Jesus Christ the Advocate is righteous as to His character and He has righteously dealt with our sins. The laver speaks of Christ in this way and the water speaks of the word.

The laver was used exclusively by priests who ministered at the altar and in the holy place. The laver was not so much a vessel at which they ministered, rather, it was a vessel that ministered unto them, supplying to them the water required for their cleansing. The thought presented by the truth of the laver is that of the need of cleansing, not so much from sin but from any kind of defilement, anything about us that is unworthy of God. Before we engage in anything which is to do with priesthood there must be time spent alone with Him that we might be cleansed. This is not here dealing primarily with confession. The laver speaks of Jesus Christ the righteous one and the water speaks of the word. It is Jesus Christ the righteous One who by the word cleanses us from defilement. There is the serious and solemn need of day by day getting alone in His presence, over God's word, that He through that word might cleanse us from everything that is unworthy of God.

Bezaleel made the laver of brass and its foot out of brazen looking glasses. The thought is that these were willingly surrendered as there was a yielding to God of that which would cater to personal vanity and pride in order that there might be fitness for the service of God. There was a willingness to divest themselves of what would glorify self and cater to one's ego in order to serve, Exod. 35. 5. The natural looking glass can never give an accurate reflection of one's true self and the practical significance is that cleansing never comes from what we see ourselves to be, but, rather, from what God sees us to be.

There was devotion on the part of the women to assist priestly men in their service to God. There are occasions when for the sake of a husband's service to God women are called upon to yield up their personal vanities. Many a servant of God has been tremendously hindered in work for God by reason of the unwillingness of a wife to yield up her personal vanities. It is good when a woman has such a high appreciation of the work of God and the importance of service to God that she is prepared thus to act before God.

Confession of sin is to be somewhat distinguished from the truth of the laver. When a believer confesses sins, the Father is faithful and just, or righteous, to forgive and cleanse those sins, 1 John 1. 9. It is worthy of note that there is no such thing before God as an unforgiven child but that forgiveness is only made good to me the moment confession is made. Today, we are never called upon to ask for forgiveness. We might have expected John to have said that the Father is 'merciful and gracious' to forgive but he says He is 'faithful and just' to forgive. He is faithful to the blood of Christ and just because of it, to grant the enjoyment of forgiveness to all His children who confess, and at the moment they do so.

Confession is often misunderstood. It is not just a half-hearted apology. The Greek word is a compound of two words meaning 'together' and 'to speak'. It may be defined as 'to speak together, to agree, to assent'. If I sin, confession involves, firstly, that I agree with God as to the wrong of the sin I have committed. Secondly, confession involves speaking. To say, 'I have not done what I should have done and I have done what I ought not to have done' is not true confession. Confession is when I tell the Father exactly what I have done and this makes it a real and bitter experience. Further, where there is confession in the New Testament, it is assumed there will be a forsaking of the sin confessed.

However, in the next chapter of John's first Epistle, in relation to the ministry of an advocate toward us, Jesus Christ is the righteous One and the propitiation for our sins. Not only has He dealt righteously with our sins when we were sinners but, by the same righteousness, He ministers to us as our advocate if we sin. The laver was made of the same copper as the altar and thus the same righteousness that demanded judgement and blood for our sins is the standard for our walk as the saints of God. Our advocate is a righteous advocate; He cannot overlook my sin or be sympathetic to it but He must deal righteously with every case and condemn everything that hinders communion.

Water is a most interesting subject. When water is viewed *en masse* it always speaks of judgement. God's gathering up all the water out of heaven into one place and the dry ground appearing speaks of the waters of judgement and the dry ground of resurrection. 'All thy waves and thy billows are gone over me', Ps. 42. 7.

Running water always speaks of the Holy Spirit. The Lord Jesus said, 'He that believeth on me, as the scripture hath said, out of his belly shall flow rivers of living water. 'But this spake he of the Spirit', John 7. 38-39.

Placid water always speaks of the word. In the laver it is not judgement, or the Holy Spirit, but the placid water that speaks of the word. 'Wherewithal shall a young man cleanse his way? by taking heed thereto according to thy word', Ps. 119. 9. 'Now ye are clean through the word which I have spoken unto you', John 15. 3. 'Christ also loved the church, and gave himself for it; that he might sanctify and cleanse it with the washing of water by the word', Eph. 5. 25-26. Thus, the water speaks of the word. To be cleansed, we need to read the word, to know it, and to quote it. This does not cleanse by itself, however, it is as we allow it to wound and to judge us, bowing under the application of the word by the Holy Spirit that it cleanses.

There are other aspects to cleansing. In 1 John chapter 3, he who has his hope set on Christ and His coming 'purifieth himself even as he is pure'. In the laver, however, it is not purification because of having hope set on Him but it is rather that the Holy One has called us and we must take character from Him. 'As he which hath called you is holy, so be ye holy', 1 Pet. 1. 15.

Its measurements

In common with such items as the lampstand and the mercy seat, no measurements are given for the laver. When the apostle Peter says, 'As he which hath called you is holy, so be ye holy in all manner of conversation', 1 Pet. 1. 15, he is indicating that we should be holy 'in every form of conduct'. Practical holiness is to have no limits. Though we shall never reach the perfection of holiness down here it is something that is to be a constant exercise as long as we are on earth. We ought never to be content with our state or our condition, but constantly endeavour to perfect holiness in the fear of God.

1 Peter chapter 1 verse 16 should read, 'Ye shall be holy; for I am holy'. Some have thought this refers to heaven because the future tense is employed but that is not the case. Peter's employment of 'shall' is to indicate that holiness for the child of God is imperative, not optional. When Peter says, 'Be ye holy; for I am holy', it is not the standard of holiness that is in view but the reason for it. Since our holiness is linked with God we understand that there are no measurements to the laver.

In Revelation chapter 4, John sees a sea of glass like unto crystal, which speaks of the holiness of God. Notice, however, that in heaven it is a sea of glass, not a sea of water. In heaven there will be no further need of cleansing; there will be no defilement and no more sin. Of course, as people of God our hearts yearn for the time when we shall see Him and never more sin against Him and never again be defiled.

71

The Laver

Finally, other vessels which were in the wilderness journey were covered, but not the laver. It seems that it could be carried without staves, possibly because of its foot. Thus, the laver was constantly open to view, a constant reminder of God's holiness.

The Golden Lampstand
Exodus 25. 31-40

Introduction

It is important to observe that there was one lampstand with its perpendicular shaft. This had six lateral branches, Exod. 25. 32, three out of each side. The lampstand and its branches were ornamented with three things: bowls, knops, flowers. There were accompanying instruments employed in connection with its use, namely tongs and snuff dishes, v. 38.

There was also the oil for the light. Both the golden lampstand and the oil are spoken of as being pure and so there was a pure lamp and pure oil used in connection with it.

Its position

In connection with the tabernacle there were three sources of light. In the camp of Israel the nation was supplied with light during the night from the pillar of fire. In the holy place, where only the priests were permitted to enter, their service was facilitated by light from the golden lampstand. Then, in the holiest of all, the high priest was provided with light by the Shekinah.

It is because this golden lampstand shines in the holy place in the interests of the priest that it does not speak of Christ as the light of the world; it was hidden from the world for the enjoyment of the priests.

The lampstand was to be positioned on the south side of the holy place. The word for south means 'bright' and 'radiant' and this is appropriate to its position.

Its material

The golden lampstand was made of pure gold, v. 31, and was perhaps the most costly of the vessels in the tabernacle. We have already noticed that in relation to the tabernacle mention is made of 'pure gold' and of 'gold'. The golden lampstand was of 'pure gold'. This vessel was made out of one piece, reminding us of that one Son, God's only begotten, unique Son. 'All of it was one beaten work of pure gold', 37. 22. No doubt Bezaleel looked upon that one piece of pure gold and in his mind's eye he would have the finished article standing in all its beauty in the holy place. This causes us to understand, however feebly, God looking upon His only begotten Son, that pure gold, giving Him and not sparing Him because of the end in view – all that His coming into the world would mean to both God and man.

There was no wood in the golden lampstand. Shittim wood speaks of humanity; gold speaks of divine righteousness; pure gold speaks of deity. Regarding pure gold, there are three persons in the Godhead. In days when our Saviour's deity is being assailed, we need to be thoroughly established in its glorious truth. The Godhead is not one person manifested in a three-fold way. There are three persons in the Godhead; the Father, the Son and the Holy Spirit and each of these persons is called 'God'. Deity belongs to each of these three persons. The Father is called God in, for example, Philippians chapter 2 verse 11; the Son of God is called God in Hebrews chapter 1 verse 8; the Holy Spirit is called God in Acts chapter 5 verse 4. There are many other references.

There is, in the lampstand, an emphasis on the deity of our blessed Saviour. In the New Testament, the word 'godhead' occurs three times in the King James Version. It is important to observe that Colossians chapter 2 verse 9 is different from the other two references. 'Godhead' in Colossians chapter 2 speaks of deity, but in Romans chapter 1 verse 20 and Acts chapter 17 verse 29 the word simply means 'pertaining to deity'. The pure gold of the lampstand speaks of the essential deity of the One who was here on earth but has now returned to heaven. Because 'divinity' means 'pertaining to deity' we are more accurate when speaking of His person to speak of His 'deity'.

The lampstand was of beaten work. There are different words for 'beating' in the Old Testament. Leviticus chapter 24 speaks of pure oil beaten for the light as does Exodus chapter 27. The word means 'to beat down' in the sense of 'crushing'. It is similar to the word used of incense 'beaten small'. The word there has the thought of 'without any consideration for ornamentation; crushing'. In regard to the golden lampstand and the mercy seat, however, the word is not that for 'beating down' but 'beating out'. The Hebrew conveys the idea of 'to produce something of tremendous value'. Thus, in regard to the golden lampstand and the mercy seat, it is not the idea of crushing regardless of resultant shape or form, but beating out skilfully so as to produce a beautiful design. In the olive beaten, or spices beaten, there is the thought of Calvary but in the golden lampstand of beaten work it is not so much the crushing of Calvary but beating to produce something wonderful, beautiful, exquisite. The thought that is conveyed is that of God's Son, the pure gold, back in heaven having passed through experiences here, the beating out, that were not proper to deity. It is wonderful to think that it was the one who was verily God who said, 'Thou didst make me hope when I was upon my mother's breasts', Ps. 22. 9, and of whom it was said, 'Jesus increased in wisdom and stature, and in favour with God and man', Luke 2. 52. He was still God and yet passed through experiences not proper to deity.

The lampstand stands in sharp contrast to the golden calf of Exodus chapter 32. That was a molten calf, of which Aaron said, Moses said, 'I cast it into the fire, and there came out this calf', 32. 24. The exquisitely proportioned and ornamented lampstand was not produced like this, or so easily, but was the product of long, skilful beating by Bezaleel, 31. 1-3, a man who was filled with divine wisdom. It must have taken hour upon hour of patient workmanship, beating it out of this one piece of pure gold. To sin is easy, but to produce something for God is another matter, demanding tremendous exercise.

No mention is made of any foundation or base for the golden lampstand. There is in view our Saviour not so much in regard to His being on earth but rather the one who was here in the fullness of the Godhead but who is now back in heaven. When we come to consider the knops and bowls we shall see that He has been here and is back in heaven having passed through experiences that were not proper to deity. This is an amazing truth. 'Though he were a Son, yet learned he obedience by the things which he suffered', Heb. 5. 8.

Its ornamentation

We have seen that there were six lateral branches, three on each side of the perpendicular shaft of the lampstand. 'And there shall be a knop under two branches of the same, and a knop under two branches of the same, and a knop under two branches of the same, according to the six branches that proceed out of the candlestick', Exod. 25. 35. A 'knop' was a bud and 'flowers' were blossoms. These six lateral branches were joined to the main perpendicular lampstand at knops on either side of its main shaft.

The perpendicular shaft has four bowls, four knops and four flowers. Four is the universal number signifying here something that has the whole world in view. Then there were six branches. Six is man's number. The six branches were divided into two: three came out of one side and three out of the other side. The number three speaks of testimony. 'In the mouth of two or three witnesses every word may be established', Matt. 18. 16. The witness is to two classes of men, one on either side, and these are Jew and Gentile. We have, therefore, a vessel speaking of the Son of God, divine provision for the whole world.

The lampstand of pure gold, beaten, speaks of the Son of God and three experiences through which He passed. In the bud is the thought of His childhood; in the blossom there is the thought of His manhood, while, in the bowls made like to almonds, there is the thought of His risen manhood. The Son of God is now back in heaven having passed through the experiences of childhood, manhood and risen manhood in this world, experiences which were not proper to deity.

We may think of these experiences of the Son of God and easily forget that He was still the Son of God when the words were fulfilled which were spoken prophetically of Him, 'Thou art he that took me out of the womb: thou didst make me hope when I was upon my mother's breasts', Ps. 22. 9. God said to Him at Bethlehem, 'Thou art my Son; this day have I begotten thee', Ps. 2. 7. 'And the child grew, and waxed strong', Luke 2. 40. At the time of His baptism He 'began to be about thirty years of age', 3. 23. He passed through death and for forty days was seen in all the wonder of His risen manhood.

The bowls were made like to almonds. Almonds speak of resurrection. In Numbers chapter 16, there is the rebellion against Moses and Aaron by the sons of Korah, Dathan and Abiram, with the two hundred and fifty princes. The earth swallowed up the sons of Korah and the fire consumed the two hundred and fifty princes. In Numbers chapter 17, the Lord commanded that a rod be given from each tribe, with their names on them, and they be placed in the tabernacle of the congregation. In the morning it was Aaron's rod that budded and blossomed and yielded almonds. Almonds thus speak of resurrection.

In these bowls was put the pure oil for the light. Though there were many cups and almonds so to speak, there were only seven lamps. Seven cups contained the oil that was set alight and the other cups, no doubt, just contained the supplies of the oil for future use. The pure oil that speaks of the Holy Spirit was contained in the almond like bowls. These bowls, speaking to us of Christ in resurrection, remind us that the Holy Spirit was not given in His fullness until Jesus had been raised and glorified. 'He that believeth on me, as the scripture hath said, out of his belly shall flow rivers of living water. (But this spake he of the Spirit, which they that believe on him should receive: for the Holy Ghost was not yet given; because that Jesus was not yet glorified)', John 7. 38-39. The Holy Spirit given is the result of the Lord Jesus Christ risen. Our Saviour said, 'It is expedient for you that I go away: for if I go not away, the Comforter will not come unto you; but if I depart, I will send him unto you', 16. 7. Peter said, 'Therefore being by the right hand of God exalted, and having received of the Father the promise of the Holy Ghost, he hath shed forth this, which ye now see and hear', Acts 2. 33. The oil is not connected therefore with the bud or the blossom but the bowls made like unto almonds, linked with the Lord's resurrection.

Its dimensions

Like the laver there are no dimensions given for the lampstand and its accessories. Its weight is given as being 'of a talent of pure gold', Exod. 25. 39. A talent is just over one hundred-weight. This does not convey the thought of Him giving the Holy Spirit without measure, as it is not the oil but the lampstand that is without measure. It is the seven lights which indicate that He giveth not the Holy Spirit by measure. However, the lack of given dimensions has the idea of fullness, that which cannot be measured, but from a different standpoint. 'In him dwelleth all the fulness of the Godhead bodily', Col. 2. 9. The pure gold cannot be measured and the lack of measurements, together with the fact that the weight was given, emphasize quality, not quantity.

The lack of measurements for the brazen laver indicates that none can measure God's holiness but in the golden lampstand that none can measure Christ's person. He is inscrutable. He said, 'All things are delivered unto me of my Father: and no man knoweth the Son, but the Father; neither knoweth any man the Father, save the Son, and he to whomsoever the Son will reveal him', Matt. 11. 27. The Son of God is inscrutable not so much because He is deity but because He is the only one in whom deity and humanity are inextricably and eternally combined.

Its lamps

It is possible that the lampstand was the tallest item of furniture but the main point would seem to be that the lampstand was designed in such a way, and the almonds that contained the oil were so skilfully positioned, as to throw the light in the direction the Holy Spirit intended. Light shone first of all against the golden lampstand itself and then to illuminate the golden altar and table of showbread. This required divine design as no man by natural wisdom could produce a light that would throw light against itself and then throw its light on the golden altar and table of showbread.

There were seven lamps, just as in Revelation chapter 4 there were seven lamps of fire burning before the throne, which are the seven spirits of God. These speak of the Holy Spirit in His fullness, not as seen in the Lord Jesus Christ when He was here but in connection with Christ now back in heaven. We live in the day of the fullness of the Holy Spirit.

The oil

'And thou shalt command the children of Israel, that they bring thee pure oil olive beaten for the light, to cause the lamp to burn always', Exod. 27. 20. The oil contained in the almond-like bowls was, therefore, pure oil. Not only was the lampstand pure but the oil was pure, 31. 8. Additionally, not only were both pure, but both were *beaten*. The olive was beaten to produce oil; the pure gold beaten to produce the pure lampstand. In the New Testament, the Lord Jesus is called 'the Holy One of God', Luke 4. 34, and, in Acts chapter 2, the apostle Peter speaks of the gift of the Holy Spirit of God. In fact, it is important to observe that when we enter into the holy place the emphasis is on purity; pure gold, the pure lamp, pure oil, the pure table and pure frankincense are all mentioned as being there.

The oil was placed in the almond shaped bowls, speaking of deity that has passed through death and resurrection, the oil coming down from a risen Christ. That which was accomplished in the days of His flesh is seen in the knop and the blossom; but the almond is Christ in resurrection. The oil is not connected with the knop; it is connected with the almond, with His being back in heaven. Oil that was crushed, the result of the death of Christ, was placed in the almond that speaks of the risen Christ to provide illumination.

The seven lamps refer to the fullness of the Holy Spirit given by a risen Christ and answer to the seven lamps before the throne in Revelation. God never gives the Spirit by measure to any of His people for He is given as a divine person to each believer. However, our Lord is the only one in whom the fullness of the Holy Spirit could be expressed.

Its light

The lampstand shone in the holy place, so this does not set forth our Saviour seen as the light of the world. There were no windows or apertures of any kind in the holy place so that all natural light was excluded. Apart from the lampstand there would have been complete darkness. In a general way, therefore, the lampstand would illuminate the entire holy place, shining on the golden covered boards, the beautiful vail into the holiest of all, the beautiful curtains on the roof with the white, blue, purple and scarlet. 'The things of God knoweth no man, but the Spirit of God', 1 Cor. 2. 11. Everything that speaks of Christ and His glories are illumined by the Holy Spirit; the habitation of God is a place of spiritual illumination.

The world knows nothing of the white linen that speaks of His spotless humanity; or of the heavenly Man seen in the blue; or of royalty in the purple and scarlet; or of the cherubim. It stands ignorant of the fact that the one who came to meet the claims of the divine throne is destined to rule over the universe. This knowledge belongs to priestly men illuminated by the Holy Spirit.

Later, particular illumination is mentioned. 'And thou shalt make the seven lamps thereof: and they shall light the lamps thereof, that they may give light over against it', Exod. 25. 37. 'It' is the lampstand. This is confirmed in Numbers chapter 8 verse 2, where the Lord says to Moses, 'When thou lightest the lamps, the seven lamps shall give light over against the candlestick'. The primary, specific function of the light was, therefore, to throw light over against the lampstand itself and the lamps were so constructed, and perhaps the wicks in them, that they illuminated the lampstand itself. The light speaks of the Holy Spirit and the lampstand speaks of Christ. The first and greatest ministry of the Holy Spirit is to glorify the Son of God, 'He shall glorify me: for he shall receive of mine, and shall shew it unto you', John 16. 14. To apprehend the glories of the Son of God is beyond the capability of mere flesh and blood; He can only be apprehended by Spirit-filled illumination.

We live in a day of the resurgence of the Pentecostal and charismatic movements, where all the emphasis is on the Holy Spirit. The test of the power of the Holy Spirit in the life of anyone is not his service, or the exercise of his gift but his appreciation of Christ. Charismatics seldom refer to the 'Lord' Jesus yet 'no man can say that Jesus is the Lord, but by the Holy Ghost', 1 Cor. 12. 3. He is seldom referred to as the Son of God, nearly always being called just 'Jesus', something which no one ever did in scripture. Some leaders went as far as to say that now we have the Spirit we can dispense with the word of God and Jesus. Nothing can be more foreign to the truth than that, and the Holy Spirit leads into all truth.

Secondly, the light from the lampstand would be thrown on the golden altar to facilitate the priest's offering up of incense on it, Exod. 30. 7-8. This is another important matter and is connected with the worship of God's people. In the light from the golden lampstand the priest would stand and minister at the golden altar. Thus, the light glorifies Christ and then facilitates worship. We have come to a time when the emphasis is on gospel activity, with social work. Alas, in many areas God is being robbed. The time for the breaking of bread is being whittled away and in some areas it is being dispensed with. Modern evangelism, with its high level of publicity, its glamour, its entertainment, and its big business has taken over so many people today. The result is that the holy, calm, contemplative worship of the breaking of bread has become unattractive to many. It is not uncommon to hear of people being involved in evangelistic activity saying that the breaking of bread and the prayer meeting are just a bore. The light for the lampstand and the incense from the golden altar were the two active matters in the holy place where the priests served; no noise was connected with either of them.

Everything should be done in a worshipful spirit, but the breaking of bread should be the high water mark. Apart from the love of Holy Scripture, the breaking of bread was the focal point of everything and the distinctive feature of assemblies. This is not the case today in many areas. The order in scripture is always worship, then service, illustrated in the Lord Jesus saying to Satan, 'Thou shalt worship the Lord thy God, and him only shalt thou serve', Luke 4. 8. In John chapter 4 our Saviour spoke first of all about worship but later to the disciples of fields white and ready to harvest. Again, in 1 Peter chapter 2 we are a holy priesthood to offer up spiritual sacrifices and then a royal priesthood to 'shew forth the praises of him who hath called you out of darkness into his marvellous light'. This principle is in evidence again at the end of the Epistle to the Hebrews: 'By him therefore let us offer the sacrifice of praise to God continually, that is, the fruit of our lips giving thanks to his name. But to do good and to communicate forget not: for with such sacrifices God is well pleased', Heb. 13. 15-16.

Thirdly, the lampstand in a particular way lit the table of shewbread. 'And he put the candlestick in the tent of the congregation, over against the table, on the side of the tabernacle southward', Exod. 40. 24. Thus, the gracious ministry of the Holy Spirit not only facilitates worship but is enlightening as to Christ, the food of His people. He has satisfied the heart of God and satisfies our hearts as well.

'The heart is satisfied; can ask no more;
All thought of self is now for ever o'er:
Christ, its unmingled object, fills the heart
In blest adoring love, its endless part', J. N. DARBY.

'And thou shalt command the children of Israel, that they bring
thee pure oil olive beaten for the light, to cause the lamp to burn
always. In the tabernacle of the congregation without the vail,
which is before the testimony, Aaron and his sons shall order it
from evening to morning before the Lord: it shall be a statute for
ever unto their generations on the behalf of the children of Israel',
Exod. 27. 20-21. The light was burning always from this pure oil,
reminding us that the Holy Spirit was given for ever. The Lord
Jesus said, 'I will pray the Father, and he shall give you another
Comforter, that he may abide with you for ever', John 14. 16.
Note, too, that it was burning from evening to morning. The Holy
Spirit is given for ever, and until the morning of His coming again
when both the Church and the Holy Spirit will be taken out of the
way as far as this world is concerned, 2 Thess. 2. 7.

The dressing of the lamps

'And the tongs thereof, and the snuffdishes thereof, shall be of
pure gold', Exod. 25. 38. The dressing of the lamps took place
every morning, 30. 7, that the light might shine the more brightly
and this brought the gold tongs and the snuffdishes into use. It
was not the oil that was dressed but the wick, which is not even
mentioned. The oil flowed to the wick to keep the oil burning.
The priests would move the ash away from the wick and put it
into a snuff box, which was a kind of censer. The wick speaks of
believers through whom the light shines as the oil flows.
Believers, then, are mentioned only by way of implication, that no
flesh might glory in His presence. The time was that when our
brethren wrote they would do so anonymously or just their initials
would be printed but now Christians advertise where they were
educated, their degrees, and their family connections. These
things have nothing to do with the service of God. It is time we

83

stopped to think in terms of 'not I but Christ'. All else is of the flesh.

An account is taken of each twenty-four hours period of our lives. These portions were not taken and thrown away; they were preserved when put into the snuffdish, the gold censer. The day is coming when we shall be confronted with each day's shining. Not only are our tears put in a bottle but each day's service and shining is in a gold snuffbox against the day of the Judgement Seat of Christ. Our daily shining for Christ will then be assessed.

Lampstands in Revelation

In Revelation chapter 2, it is not the removal of the charred wick that is in view but of the lampstand itself. That is, another lampstand in addition to Zechariah chapter 4.

In Revelation chapter 1, there are seven golden lampstands, each on its own base, which were seven assemblies in Asia. Strictly speaking, the thought is not that they shine in the world but that they are connected with the sanctuary. The golden lampstand is the value of the assembly God-ward. In the midst is the Son of Man moving, praising, condemning. He says to Ephesus, 'Remember therefore from whence thou art fallen, and repent, and do the first works; or else I will come unto thee quickly, and will remove thy candlestick out of his place, except thou repent', Rev. 2. 5. The reference is to its being removed from its place in the sanctuary as a golden lampstand; it would cease to be a golden lampstand in its value God-ward. It does not mean that the saints will be dispersed and the doors closed; it might even expand but no longer be a golden lampstand God-ward. This is very solemn.

The Table of Shewbread
Exodus 25. 23-30; Leviticus 24. 5-9

The table of showbread is termed 'the table of shewbread', Num. 4. 7, and 'a Table', Exod. 25. 23. In Hebrews chapter 9 verse 2 the language is a little different; it is termed, 'the table and his shewbread'.

Its position

'And he put the table in the tent of the congregation, upon the side of the tabernacle northward, without the vail', Exod. 40. 22. The golden lampstand was in the holy place on the south side whilst the table of shewbread was opposite to it on the north side. The shewbread is thus connected with the holy place. It is to be distinguished from the manna, which lay upon the face of the wilderness, the bread of the mighty giving strength for the wilderness pilgrimage. In contrast, the loaves were set upon a pure table, Lev. 24. 9, beneath the light of the lampstand, and were the bread of the priests, the bread of communion connected with their service in the holy place. We shall need to keep this in mind to be consistent in our interpretation.

The table speaks of fellowship and, primarily, of fellowship with God. The bread on the table was the shewbread, the bread of faces; it was laid before the face of God and was before Him always, but on the Sabbath it was taken off and eaten by the priests. It was on the table, first of all, for the heart of God; then, the priests had fellowship as they fed upon that which in the first instance had satisfied God's heart. In that the table was not in the court or the camp but in the holy place, we are reminded of the important truth that we must see to it that holy things are never made common. Holy things were to be partaken of in a holy place.

Its material

'Thou shalt also make a table of shittim wood: two cubits shall be the length thereof, and a cubit the breadth thereof, and a cubit and a half the height thereof. And thou shalt overlay it with pure gold, and make thereto a crown of gold round about', Exod. 25. 23-24. It was, therefore, made of shittim wood overlaid, in a wonderful way, with pure gold, reminding us that deity and humanity were perfectly blended in our blessed Lord. Shittim wood refers to humanity in a general way and this includes believers, who are spoken of in the boards overlaid with gold. It has a special significance when speaking of the Lord Jesus Christ personally. 'God was manifest in the flesh', 1 Tim. 3. 16, involves the idea of the shittim wood, as does 'the Word was made flesh', John 1. 14, 'God sending his own Son in the likeness of sinful flesh', Rom. 8. 3, 'God sent forth his Son, made of a woman', Gal. 4. 4, and 'as the children are partakers of flesh and blood, he also himself likewise took part of the same', Heb. 2. 14.

Pure gold speaks of His deity. In Him deity and humanity are combined inextricably and eternally. Of only One is this true and this is what makes the Son of God to be inscrutable. God indwells man by the Holy Spirit but only the Son of God became man. The shittim wood and the pure gold could never be separated. It is important not to seek to divide between His manhood and His deity. Our Lord was not part man and part God; He was wholly man and wholly God and, at the same time, one glorious person.

The order is shittim wood overlaid with gold. The fact that the shittim wood was not seen indicates that it is not Christ here on earth that is in view. When He was here it was shittim wood that was predominantly seen but now it is Christ up there, overlaid within and without with pure gold. Let us remember, however, that the shittim wood is still there. He has taken His risen manhood back to heaven and to the throne of God. Indeed, He will never cease to be man. Speaking of Christ now at God's right hand, the apostle says, 'In him dwelleth all the fulness of the Godhead bodily', Col. 2. 9.

Its measurements

The table of shewbread measured two cubits in length, one cubit in breadth and one and a half cubits in height. Two cubits speaks of testimony; one cubit speaks of what is unique. The table was the same height as the ark with the mercy seat on it and, since the brazen altar and altar were three cubits high, and the grating was in the midst of it, that grating on which the sacrifice was laid was also at the same height. These three things at the same height of one and a half cubits indicate that the sacrifice of the altar is equal to the claims of the throne and has provided the basis for fellowship between God and man at the table of shewbread.

Its design

The table had *two crowns*. 'And thou shalt overlay it with pure gold, and make thereto a crown of gold round about. And thou shalt make unto it a border of an hand breadth round about, and thou shalt make a golden crown to the border thereof round about', Exod. 25. 24-25. In verse 24 the *table* was crowned but in verse 25 its *border* was crowned.

These two crowns signify in a beautiful way matters spoken of in the prayer of God's Son in John chapter 17. He spoke of a two-fold glory when He said, 'glorify thy Son', v. 1, and 'glorify thou me', v. 5. Verse 1 is couched in impersonal language, which continues in verse 2. He is speaking as the subject Son and the glory about which He prayed is the Father's answer to what the Son had done for Him down here. He said, 'I have glorified thee on the earth', v. 4. This is, therefore, an acquired, additional glory and connects with the border crown; in that the border was added and it was crowned, there is seen the acquired glory of the subject Son. In verse 5, however, He said, 'glorify thou me'. This is the table itself; it is divine glory and the Son resumes a position of glory that was His by right.

He will, of course, never impart to us His divine, eternal glory. The language of John chapter 17 verse 24 is, 'Father, I will that they also, whom thou hast given me, be with me where I am; that they may behold my glory, (His eternal glory) which thou hast given me (as to its position): for thou lovedst me before the foundation of the world'. He cannot share that with us. He may share with us the glory of verse 1 but not of verse 5. The glory He shares with us is His acquired glory and is connected with His kingdom, 'that they might be perfected into one that the world may know that thou hast sent me, and thou hast loved them, as thou hast loved me', v. 23 JND. The world shall know this when we appear with Christ in His shared glory. However, the glory of verse 5 is that of verse 24; it is a glory He cannot share and one the world will never see. The glory we shall behold is the glory pictured in the crown of the table, a glory exclusively His. He calls it, 'my glory'.

Between both of these crowns, on each side of the table, was a *border*. There was, therefore, a crown, then a border, and then the second crown. The border measured a handbreadth and it is remarkable to notice that between verses 1 and 5 of John chapter 17 there are four mentions of a giving hand in which the Father gives and the Son gives. This is not insignificant. Firstly, the Father gives work to the Son. He says to the Father, 'I have glorified thee on the earth: I have finished the work which thou gavest me to do', v. 4. Thus, one crown relates to a finished work on the handbreadth of the borders. Secondly, a crown on another side is seen in verse 2 when the Son speaks to the Father about the authority over all flesh that He had given Him. Thirdly, the Father gives to the Son many sons, whilst the crown on the fourth side is the gift of eternal life that He should give to as many as the Father has given Him. Here, then, is the handbreadth on the four sides of the table.

The border gave security to the twelve loaves as they were not removed even in transit: 'thou shalt set upon the table shewbread before me alway', Exod. 25. 30.

Mention is made of *rings and staves* in verses 26-28 and we are told the purpose for which they were made, namely that the table may be borne with them. The rings and staves were necessary when the tabernacle was in transit in the wilderness journey. Therefore, the loaves were not only secure but were also assured of support.

The rings were made of gold and the staves of shittim wood overlaid with gold. The rings speak of the promise of the eternal God. The staves remind us of the support of God's Son in whom is combined deity and humanity; He is Son of Man and Son of God.

The staves indicate the wilderness character of the table. There were no staves in the temple as the pilgrim character of the people was then over. As with the ark, when it was taken into the temple the staves were drawn out for the first time ever.

Verse 29 mentions the 'dishes thereof'. The *dishes* were to remove the bread when it was to be eaten. There were also *spoons*, which were used for spreading frankincense on the bread. In addition, there were covers to cover the table. Verse 29 again speaks of 'bowls to cover withal' or 'pour out withal' (margin). These *bowls* were no doubt connected with the drink offering. All these accessories were of pure gold, indicating that divine things are divinely appropriated.

The twelve loaves on the table

The *preparation of the loaves* must have been in the houses of the children of Israel, who had to bring them by an everlasting covenant. Thus, the people made what rested on the table as the food of the priests. It shows how necessary it is that in our homes there are conditions in which we can produce something that speaks of Christ.

The loaves, as food for the priests, represent the person of our Lord Jesus Christ. 'And thou shalt take fine flour, and bake twelve cakes thereof: two tenth deals shall be in one cake', Lev. 24. 5. The loaves were baked and then pure frankincense was put on the bread for a memorial, see v. 7. There is perpetual fragrance even now from the person of Christ in heaven. He fills heaven with the fragrance of His own person. Fine flour speaks of our Saviour's holy manhood. The fact that it was baked and pierced signifies that He passed through the fire and went into death. The loaves were then put on the table, reminding us of the man now in heaven, the Holy One having passed through death but now exalted. The fire was not, of course, to arrest the activity of leaven, for in sacrifices that speak of Christ there was none.

The loaves were made of *fine flour*. I feel that the fineness of the flour was not produced by grinding but the flour was in itself *inherently* fine. It takes grinding to produce fineness in us, as we experience the circumstances of life with its hardships. Circumstances never produced anything in Christ; He was inherently fine and circumstances only revealed what was already there. This is reminiscent of the fine twined linen. Everything about our Lord was fine. The flour was not white (it needs to be bleached for that) but it was fine. His manhood was holy, but fineness speaks of even texture. Every grace and characteristic was perfect, none finer than the other, His holiness being not greater than His love or His purity greater than His grace.

'Two tenth deals (of flour) shall be in one cake', v. 5. An omer of manna was laid up before the Lord, Exod. 16. 33, an omer being the tenth part of an ephah. Thus, there was in one loaf double the amount that there was in the manna that was laid up. Each loaf had two-tenth deals or two omers, a double portion. The one omer of manna and the two omers in each loaf indicate the difference between the pilgrims and the priest.

'And thou shalt set upon the table shewbread before me alway', Exod. 25. 30. The purpose of the table was simply that these twelve loaves might be placed upon it. The table speaks of communion and sustenance. David said of Mephibosheth, 'He shall eat at my table, as one of the king's sons', 2 Sam. 9. 11. 'My table' is sustenance; 'my sons' is communion. 'Ye cannot be partakers of the Lord's table, and of the table of devils', 1 Cor . 10. 21. The idea of partaking is the idea of fellowship. One cannot be committed to the fellowship of the Lord's table and, at the same time, be committed to the fellowship of the table of demons.

It has already been noted that the bread was the *food of the priests* and in that respect was different from the manna. 'And it shall be Aaron's and his sons'; and they shall eat it in the holy place: for it *is* most holy unto him of the offerings of the Lord made by fire by a perpetual statute', Lev. 24. 9. In fact, the bread was to be eaten not in 'the' holy place but in 'a' holy place; that is, in the precincts of the tabernacle. Divine things can only be enjoyed in a holy atmosphere. Today, increasingly, holy things are becoming common. There is a tendency to mix the holy and common, the clean and the unclean, just as when in Malachi chapter 1 the people offered polluted bread and diseased animals.

When Aaron is seen alone as the high priest, he typifies our Lord Jesus but, when viewed as one of the priestly family, the family is a type of the believers of this present day constituted as a priesthood. This becomes clear, for example, in the consecration of the priesthood in Leviticus chapter 8 and Exodus chapter 29. When Aaron was anointed by himself he was anointed without life being sacrificed; no blood was sprinkled on Aaron when he was anointed by himself. Moses then poured oil upon him in rich profusion. That is the thought in Psalm 133, the holy anointing oil upon his head and his beard that ran down to the skirts of his garments. When he was anointed with the family, however, it was different. Before they were anointed with oil, they were sprinkled by blood. Aaron did not need to be sprinkled by blood as he speaks of our great High Priest, holy and undefiled, but the family, speaking of believers, were sprinkled by blood. Another difference is that when the family was anointed with oil it was not poured upon them, it was sprinkled. Interestingly, Luke tells us that at our Lord's baptism the Holy Spirit descended in bodily form as of a dove. This speaks of completeness. In Acts 2 when the Holy Spirit descended on the day of Pentecost, He descended as 'tongues'. This is the difference between rich profusion and sprinkling.

There were *twelve loaves* indicating that no matter the strife and division that might be in the camp outside, this food was assured for all. The priests ate them as representing the twelve tribes. There might be serious disorder and disarray out in the camp but in the holy place on the table of shewbread the loaves were set in order, Lev. 24. 8, just as, no matter the state or condition of the twelve tribes, the high priest bore in his heart in the breastplate of judgement those twelve stones on which were the names of the twelve tribes of Israel. Those priests were what God intended the whole nation to be and what the whole nation shall in fact be, a kingdom of priests.

On the shoulders of the priests, on onyx stones, were two rows of six names of the children of Israel. These were in order according to their birth but on the breastplate the order was according to their tribe. Thus, Reuben was first on the shoulder but Judah was first on the breastplate. We observe that it is our new birth that places us upon His shoulders, the place occupied by the lost sheep. Now, here is the food of a priestly people divided into two rows of six. I would suggest that six is man's number, Revelation chapter 13 makes this clear, but there were two rows of six. Two speaks of testimony. On the shoulders it was the testimony of His ability to save; on the table it is a testimony to the satisfaction of the need of the human heart. It is not here strength for human weakness, it is rather the satisfying of human need. There is complete and eternal satisfaction in that in which the loaves speak.

O what is all that earth can give
To one who shares in God's own joy:
Dead to the world, in Thee I live,
In Thee is bliss without alloy

The loaves, Lev. 24. 8, were removed and eaten every Sabbath and were replaced so that the table was never empty. As a priestly people our food is assured.

'When all created streams are dry Thy fulness is the same'

In that they were eaten on the Sabbath there is a dispensational thought in respect of the children of Israel. The Sabbath speaks of the future millennial reign when, as a priestly people, they shall feed on Christ. As far as we are concerned, we must be in the enjoyment of God's rest to feed on Christ. Communion and sustenance is never enjoyed in conditions of uncertainty, anxiety, or lack of assurance. All that answers to the Sabbath must be true in our spiritual experience to feed upon these loaves.

The manna fell daily except on the Sabbath. It was eaten on the Sabbath but not collected on the Sabbath as the day before the Sabbath the manna had to be gathered twice as much. Again, there is a dispensational thought regarding the millennium. The manna is the food for pilgrims for six days but the shewbread was for those six days before the face of God. It did not lie like the manna on the face of the wilderness, daily, for the food of the people, but lay before the face of God firstly for His satisfaction.

Manna in the wilderness signifies Christ in humiliation, whereas manna in the golden pot is Christ in exaltation but as a memorial of the one who was here. The shewbread was baked and then put on the table, typifying the exalted Man in heaven, with fragrance upon Him for the heart of God, at God's right hand. On this the priests fed, and we feed on that which has first of all satisfied the heart of God. In view here is not so much their offering to God as the fact that the loaves lay there and then the priests fed upon them. That is the highest aspect of communion.

The loaves were also for a memorial, as was the Passover and the meal offering. They speak of what is a continual memorial God-ward, before the face of God. This is true of Christ; He is before God an everlasting memorial.

The priests did not eat the *frankincense* on the loaves. We are not to think that the loaves were piled on top of one another; there was frankincense on each loaf as they lay in *two rows*, and its fragrance rose before the face of God. For six days the holy place was filled with that fragrance, before the loaves were eaten by the priests. As with the meal offering the frankincense was for God. There is a difference, however, in that in the meal offering the frankincense was all burnt, but with the shewbread there is in view the one who has passed through death and whose suffering is now past. Here is communion at the highest level; it is feeding on that which has firstly satisfied the heart of God. In worship we present to God the divine assessment of His Son, the pleasure He found in Him. At His baptism the Father indicated what the Son was to Him when He said, 'Thou art my beloved Son', Mark 1. 11. He was the object of His love and found all delight in Him, the object of His pleasure. But at the mount of transfiguration the Father said, 'This is my beloved Son in whom I am well pleased; hear ye Him', Matt. 17. 5, indicating that the Father's desire is that we should share His delight in His Son. Christ is to God 'elect' and 'precious', 1 Pet. 2. 6, and 'to you who believe He is precious', v. 7. In John 6 our Saviour is the 'bread of God' but He is also the bread God as given us to eat. As the bread of God He satisfies the heart of God and that same bread is given to us to eat.

Two other matters require comment. In 1 Samuel 21, in eating the shewbread David did what was permitted to him as an exception only. The Lord justified David in doing that when the Pharisees accused him of breaking the Sabbath. In this there is a dispensational thought. David ate of the shewbread when the king was in rejection, pointing forward to the time when the King (Christ) is in rejection and all that pertains to the temple or tabernacle is in abeyance.

Secondly, the one loaf of 1 Corinthians 10 does not represent the one body as is often taught. The passage is self-explanatory. 'For we *being* many are one bread, *and* one body' and the reason is 'for we are all partakers of that one bread', 1 Cor. 10. 17. Thus, the oneness of the body is not expressed in the one loaf but by *all partaking of that one loaf*. The one loaf does not represent the one body but it is symbolized and expressed by all partaking of it.

This is the same as Exodus chapter 12 where they were to take 'a lamb for an house'. There were many houses and many lambs but it speaks of 'the lamb'; they were viewed as one assembly and one lamb.

The Golden Altar
Exodus 30. 1-10

It has already been noted that the golden lampstand was on the south side of the holy place and the table of shewbread was on the north side. The golden altar completes the vessels that were in the holy place.

Its position

The importance of the golden altar can be understood when we see its central position in the holy place. It was 'before the vail', Exod. 30. 6, and 'before the ark of the testimony', 40. 5, and was the last vessel passed by the high priest on the Day of Atonement as he entered the holiest of all.

In fact, the golden altar was a link between the holy place, the court and the holiest, within the vail. The fire on the golden altar was brought from the brazen altar in the court, Lev. 12-13; Num. 16. 46; this was hallowed fire from heaven and all other fire was strange fire. On the Day of Atonement fire was taken in to the holiest from the golden altar, in a golden censer, and the spices that were used as incense on the golden altar, were burned in the holiest by the high priest on the live coals that were in the censer.

This appears to be the reason why the golden altar is not mentioned in Hebrews chapter 9, the background to which is the Day of Atonement, though reference is made there to the golden censer. It is important to observe that Hebrews chapter 9 does not say that the golden censer was in the holiest of all as if that was its permanent place. The language is accurate when it says of the holiest of all, 'which had the golden censer'. It is indicating that it was used in connection with the holiest on the Day of Atonement.

Reference to the golden altar is not until Exodus chapter 30, which might seem a little strange. In chapter 28 we have the garment of the priest, in chapter 29 the consecration of the priesthood and in chapter 30 the golden altar. In chapters 25-27 we read of the vessels of display, associated with God coming out to man, whereas in chapter 30 we read of the vessels of approach, associated with man going in to God. In chapters 25-27 the priest must have somewhat to offer but in chapter 30 he must have somewhere to offer. The golden altar is, therefore, the first vessel mentioned after the consecration of the priests and the first vessel mentioned in connection with man's going in to God, which again suggests its importance.

Its purpose

Its purpose was to burn incense and this is mentioned before its material, its dimensions, its position, or its design, indicating that this is the most important matter.

All, of course, speaks of God's Son. When we considered the brazen altar we saw that He is the altar, the priest, the offerer and the sacrifice and now, as we think of the golden altar, speaking of our Lord's priestly ministry in the presence of God, He is the altar, the high priest and the incense. Christ is all!

The holy anointing oil and the incense were both made from spices but with the difference that oil and spices were connected with the holy anointing oil but fire and spices were connected with the incense. The oil makes the spices applicable to us in terms of the anointing but the fire causes the incense of the spices to ascend. The perfume was wholly for the nostrils of the Lord, 30. 37-38; the people were not to make it for themselves.

As the altar, He is the *place*. As the high priest He is the *person*. As the incense He is the *perfume*, v. 35.

The place

As to its *material* the golden altar was made of shittim wood, v. 1, and pure gold, v. 3. This speaks of the priestly ministry of our Saviour. 'We have a great high priest, that is passed into the heavens, Jesus the Son of God', Heb. 4. 14. The shittim wood speaks of Jesus; the pure gold speaks of the Son of God. This opens up a big subject. In Hebrews chapter 1, He is the Son of God; in chapter 2, He is Jesus; in chapter 4, He is Jesus the Son of God.

As to its *dimensions* the golden altar was one cubit long by one cubit broad by two cubits high, Exod. 30. 2. Perhaps the fact that the length and breadth are each one cubit has the thought of there being one mediator; and, as two is a number of testimony, the height of two cubits might suggest the fact that the one mediator was to be testified in due time.

As to its *design* the golden altar, which speaks of the high priestly ministry of our Lord Jesus Christ, was *foursquare,* v. 2. It is rather like the breastplate in the garments of the high priest, which was foursquare, 'being doubled', Exod. 28. 16, into a kind of pocket. Twelve stones were put into the pocket. The thought in the altar and the breastplate being foursquare is that here is something for all the saints equally and without exception. The priestly ministry of Jesus the Son of God is not restricted to a few, or to any particular company or companies, or the aggregate of certain companies of the Lord's people to the exclusion of others. It extends to all the saints of God. In Hebrews chapter 10, He is a great priest over the house of God which is comprised of all who are living stones, born again by the Spirit of God.

The altar had *four horns.* These were not for beasts as was the case with the brazen altar because the golden altar was not connected with involuntary sacrifice. Rather, they speak of *power* resident in our great High Priest at God's right hand in heaven. In Hebrews, He is able to succour in chapter 2, He is able to sympathize in chapter 4 and He is able to save in chapter 7.

The fact that they were four in number indicates that the power of Christ's present high priestly ministry is available for all. Our Lord's priestly ministry always has in view the saints' approach to the throne and so His people are encouraged to 'come boldly unto the throne of grace', Heb. 4. 16. 'He is able also to save them to the uttermost that come (that are coming) unto God by him', 7. 25. Our approach to God is the outcome of His priestly ministry.

The altar also had a *crown of gold*, reminding us that our high priest has 'passed into (or through) the heavens', 4. 14, and who is 'higher than the heavens', 7. 26. We may distinguish Hebrews chapter 2 verse 9, which speaks of the fact that He is crowned with glory and honour, in that this relates not to His priesthood but the present pledge of His future dominion.

It also had *rings and staves* 'to bear it withal', Exod. 30. 4-5. When the camp was moving and the tabernacle was in transit, the golden altar was with them, borne by rings and staves. This indicates that as our great High Priest Christ is always with us and available. This connects to Hebrews chapter 4, where we learn that there is grace to help in every time of need.

The person

'And Aaron shall burn thereon sweet incense every morning: when he dresseth the lamps, he shall burn incense upon it. And when Aaron lighteth the lamps at even, he shall burn incense upon it, a perpetual incense before the Lord throughout your generations', Exod. 30. 7-8.

Our Lord is seen here as 'a minister of the sanctuary, and of the true tabernacle, which the Lord pitched, and not man', Heb. 8. 2. In Hebrews chapter 1 our Lord has a more excellent name, whereas in chapter 8 He has a more excellent ministry. Aaron ministering before the Lord at the golden altar would speak of our Lord as the High Priest and Minister of the sanctuary. It is precious to think that in the true tabernacle, which the Lord pitched and not men, we have a High Priest who is there as a minister of the sanctuary and on our behalf. We are encouraged in Hebrews chapter 13 verse 15 to 'offer the sacrifice of praise to God continually, that is, the fruit of *our* lips giving thanks to his name', and, in 1 Peter chapter 2 verse 5, we are reminded that we are a holy priesthood 'to offer up spiritual sacrifices, acceptable to God by Jesus Christ'. However, what we present to God in worship must first of all be holy to us, verse 37, 'unto thee holy for the Lord'. This would set us free from lightness and irreverence.

In Leviticus chapter 9, God sent fire down and this had to be kept burning, Lev. 6. This was the hallowed fire and they were not to offer strange or unhallowed fire, that is, fire that did not burn on the brazen altar. The *fire* on the golden altar was a slow burning process. The head, skin, legs, inwards, and dung of offerings were burnt outside the camp with a quick, devouring flame; they were speedily put out of sight by being burnt to ashes, but here the slow burning of the incense was to produce fragrance.

Every *morning* Aaron dressed the lamps and burned incense and every *evening* he lit them and again burned incense. The incense in the morning marked the commencement of another day and the incense in the evening marked its end. The day, therefore, began and ended with what speaks of Christ. Incense would perpetually ascend, burning all day and all night, priestly responsibility being concerned with what speaks of Christ at the beginning and end of the day. Light and incense were the two active but silent matters in the tabernacle. The light was thrown on the golden altar to facilitate the offering up of the incense. The light speaks of the illumination of the Holy Spirit and the incense of the fragrance of Christ. The light and the incense go together. For the light to shine clearly the lamps had to be daily dressed. This indicates that in respect of our worship there should be daily freshness. The charred piece was taken away for clearer light to shine on the ascending incense.

There were various things that were done morning and evening. The morning and evening sacrifice involved the lamb for the burnt offering, flour for a meal offering and a hin of wine for a drink offering. Also, the lamps were attended morning and evening and incense was offered. In Exodus chapter 30 verse 7, the order is 'morning and evening', whereas in Genesis chapter 1 it is 'evening and morning'. This is how God Himself works. He brings light out of darkness.

The perfume

The *composition* of the incense is detailed in verse 34. 'And the Lord said unto Moses, Take unto thee sweet spices, stacte, and onycha, and galbanum; *these* sweet spices with pure frankincense: of each shall there be a like *weight'*. All speaks of the Lord Jesus Christ ascending to God as worship. Worship is a presentation of Christ to God; God delights in Him and so should we. The holy place was thus filled with the odour of the incense, just as in John chapter 12 the house was filled with the odour of Mary's ointment.

Of the four ingredients of the incense the first three go together but the fourth, the frankincense, is unique. Frankincense is always wholly for God. Stacte means 'to drop or distil'. Christ's gracious words distilled as the dew, Deut. 32. 2. Onycha means 'lion' and reminds us of the majesty of His person. Galbanum means 'fat', reminding us of His inward excellence. The frankincense means 'white' and reminds us of His external purity.

There was to be *a like weight* of each ingredient teaching us that in the Lord Jesus Christ no grace outshines another. The ingredients of the incense were 'tempered together' reminding us of the perfect blend of all His graces, not one conflicting with another. There are two different words for 'beating' in the Old Testament. In respect of the mercy seat and the golden lampstand the word used means 'to beat to produce something wonderful or exquisite' but in respect of the incense the word carries the idea of 'beating down, crushing and making small'.

We should note the *descriptions* of the incense. It is called 'sweet incense', Exod. 30. 7, pure and holy, v. 35, and most holy, v. 36. All speaks of the person of Christ being sweet, pure, and most holy. We can never assess the sweetness of Christ to the heart of God. He is pleased to call Him 'my servant, whom I uphold; mine elect, in whom my soul delighteth', Isa. 42. 1, and 'my beloved Son', Matt. 3. 17. In that He was pure we remember that we, defiled by sin, cannot properly appreciate what it meant to God that an impeccably holy Man was here and is now in His presence. He was most holy, not in the sense that He did not or would not sin but that He could not sin. This is impeccability. He was untarnished by sin and unmixed by evil but He was most holy in this respect, that His holiness was impeccable; it was impossible for Him to sin.

In the holy place there was pure gold, pure oil, pure incense and a pure table. Everything there spoke of the Holy One of God. Anything sullied or tainted could never speak of the Lord Jesus Christ or the Holy Spirit.

The Vail
Exodus 26. 31-35

Its position

'And thou shalt hang up the vail under the taches, that thou mayest bring in thither within the vail the ark of the testimony: and the vail shall divide unto you between the holy *place* and the most holy', v. 33. The taches are the taches of gold that joined the two sets of the five beautiful curtains which we have already considered and thus they were hung up under the taches. I believe that they were hung up by hooks on the taches themselves.

The vail divided between the holy place and the most holy. The word 'vail' means 'to conceal or to hide' and thus the vail shut God in. We have already seen that there was the gate, see Exod. 27. 16, through which a redeemed people could enter as far as the brazen altar. We have also considered the door of the tent, 26. 37, through which the priestly family, not the common Israelite, could enter to attend the lampstand, the table, and the altar. The vail, however, does not convey the thought of entry as does the gate and the door; it signifies 'to separate' or 'to screen'. The idea in the vail is not of entry so much as shutting God in, and separating between the holiest and the holy place. After Nadab and Abihu drew nigh to God presumptuously, without authority and with unhallowed fire, and were devoured by fire that went out from the Lord, entry through the vail into the holiest was restricted to one day each year, the Day of Atonement, and limited to the high priest. 'But into the second, the high priest only once a year, not without blood, which he offers for himself, and *for* the errors of the people', Heb. 9. 7 JND. Thus, the redeemed went through the gate, the priestly family went through the door but the *high priest alone* went within the vail.

Something not commonly understood is that God spoke to Moses in the holy of holies and it is evident that Moses had entry there. 'And when Moses was gone into the tabernacle of the congregation to speak with him, then he heard the voice of one speaking unto him from off the mercy seat that *was* upon the ark of testimony, from between the two cherubims: and he spake unto him', Num. 7. 89. In Leviticus we have the expression, 'And the Lord called unto Moses' or 'And the Lord said unto Moses' repeatedly and these were occasions where the Lord spoke to Moses from off the mercy seat. God spoke to Moses on the occasion of the burning bush and on Mount Sinai, but now that the tabernacle is reared He spoke to Moses from off the mercy seat.

However, after the death of Moses the holiest became completely silenced. The priests would enter in the holy place daily to attend to the morning and evening sacrifices, to attend the lamp and the altar, and weekly to attend the table. 'The priests went always into the first tabernacle, accomplishing the service *of God'*, Heb. 9. 6. While the footsteps of the priests could be heard as they served in the holy place not a sound would be heard from behind the vail. How solemn and awful must that silence have been! God dwelt in an atmosphere that must not be disturbed. When Aaron entered (as a type of our Lord Jesus Christ as our High Priest) that vail covered the full width of the sanctuary, completely screening the holy of holies. The vail made clear that here was one spot on earth where God's priests must not put a foot.

The prime purpose of the vail in the tabernacle, therefore, was that it would divide between what belonged to the high priest who represented Christ and where he ministered and what belongs to the priestly family (who represent believers) and where they ministered. It hid the ark, Exod. 40. 3, and repeatedly the vail is spoken of as 'the vail of the covering', see 35. 12; 39. 34; 40. 21. Once the ark was placed in the holiest it was not intended to be seen except by the high priest on the Day of Atonement.

Even in transit, the ark was not to be seen. 'And when the camp setteth forward, Aaron shall come, and his sons, and they shall take down the covering vail, and cover the ark of testimony with it', Num. 4. 5. The ark was so holy, so shut in and covered that Aaron and his sons would take down the vail from its hooks and then walk in towards the ark and cover it without casting an eye upon it. Thus, the vail was not so much a means of entry but a screen or a covering, and so symbolized divine dealings with Israel as a nation, namely 'that the way into the holiest of all was not yet made manifest, while as the first tabernacle was yet standing', Heb. 9. 8.

Its pillars

This vail was supported by four pillars of shittim wood which were overlaid with gold and stood on four sockets of silver. Their hooks were of gold. The gate was also supported by four pillars. This might refer to the four evangelists. The door into the holy place was supported by five pillars and this could refer to the five writers of the epistles.

The vail, supported by four pillars, refers again to Matthew, Mark, Luke and John but there is now a difference in that the four pillars of the gate were differently constructed from the pillars connected to the vail. In respect of the gate we are not told what the pillars were made of, although they had sockets of copper and hooks of silver; the emphasis is on their use for the hanging of the beautiful gate. With those pillars the idea is 'not I but Christ'. In respect of the four pillars of the vail, they are stated to be made of wood overlaid with gold, which is the same as the boards of the tabernacle structure proper. These speak of the believer having a standing in divine righteousness. Here we have the four Evangelists, not so much in relation to their testimony to the world as in respect of the gate but, rather, associated with the habitation of God.

The pillars supporting the vail were on sockets of silver, which speaks of the preciousness of the price paid for redemption. This indicates that they were standing not so much on an appreciation of one who sustained the fire (as seen in the four pillars of the gate standing on sockets of copper) but on an appreciation of the preciousness of the price paid for the ransom.

The four pillars of the gate had hooks of silver on which the gate was suspended whereas the four pillars on which the vail was hung had hooks of gold and this suggests that the presentation of Christ by the four evangelists can be seen from two standpoints. The gate speaks of the presentation of Christ to the world and the fact that its hooks were of silver, speaking of the price of redemption, indicates that this presentation is because of what He wrought for them at Calvary. In connection with the vail, however, the presentation is connected not to hooks of silver but of gold; what they had to say was divine in its origin and character. This is not the preaching of Christ to the world as meeting its need but the presentation of the person of Christ to priestly men for their appreciation. The pillars were not seen by the priestly men, of course, but what they presented was seen and in that is the divine, unique inspiration of the four evangelists in their presentation by the Holy Spirit of the person of Christ.

Its material

'And thou shalt make a vail *of* blue, and purple, and scarlet, and fine twined linen of cunning work: with cherubims shall it be made', Exod. 26. 31. This was the same as the beautiful curtains but with the difference, v. 1, that in regard to the beautiful curtains the fine twined linen is mentioned first but in the vail the blue is mentioned first and fine twined linen is last. As the priests looked up on the beautiful curtains they would see, symbolically in the linen, the Holy One who was here, and, in the purple and scarlet, the one who has gone back to heaven and is destined to reign. But, when they approached the vail, the blue comes first and thus approach into the holiest is connected to God's Son predominantly where He is now. '*Having* an high priest over the house of God; let us draw near', Heb. 10. 21-22.

There are many different things suggested by the colours but they all speak of Christ. The daughters of Midian were clothed with purple which, as the book of Esther indicates, is the colour of Gentile royalty. Scarlet is the colour of Jewish royalty. Purple speaks of the Son of Man with universal dominion, whilst scarlet speaks of the Son of David whose dominion is in regard to the nation of Israel. Scarlet is worm scarlet; the one who will yet fill the throne must first have filled the altar, where He became a worm and not a man, Ps. 22. 6.

We might ask as to how the vail with its various colours speak of Christ as shutting man out and shutting God in. In the gate there were no cherubim. As they passed through the gate people were introduced to the brazen altar, which suggests something that is all of grace. In the vail, however, there are cherubim and here is Christ associated with the righteous character of God. Entering into God's presence there must be an appreciation of divine righteousness and divine requirements must be satisfied. Fine linen speaks to us of practical righteousness as we have seen but the cherubim speak of the judicial action of the throne of God. When we think of our Lord Jesus Christ, we think of One, and only One, against whom divine righteousness could make no claim, not one just accusation whatsoever. He is the one exception to Ecclesiastes chapter 7 verse 20, 'For *there is* not a just man upon earth, that doeth good, and sinneth not', and, to Romans chapter 3 verse 10, 'There is none righteous, no, not one'. In that vail of blue, purple, scarlet, fine twined linen in which were the cherubim we see one who is Himself the glory of God, the only One who could meet the requirements of God's throne.

The rent vail

The vail of the temple was rent in the Gospels but in Hebrews, where the background is the tabernacle, the vail remains intact. There is no rent vail in that epistle.

The rending of the vail is mentioned three times in the Gospels, in Matthew 27, Mark 15 and Luke 23. Matthew and Mark record the historical order in the rending of the vail but Luke records the moral order. The vail was rent at the ninth hour, Matt. 27. 50-51; Mark 15. 37-38, and Matthew and Mark tell us it was consequent upon our Lord yielding up the ghost, but Luke records that it was when the sun was darkened. That event symbolized the moral state of the world which, at that time, condemned this righteous man; the sun being darkened is the reason why the centurion said 'Certainly this was a righteous man', Luke 23. 47. Thus, Luke tells us that the vail was rent before He gave up the ghost, vv. 44-46. This symbolized that heaven was opened to receive the spirit of this righteous person.

'Where the word of a king *is, there is* power', Eccles. 8. 4. When our Lord cried with a loud voice in Matthew it is the voice of a king. Here is the evidence of His voice of authority: the sun darkened, the rocks rent, the graves opened and the saints arose. These signs, in the Gospel of a Jewish background, prove that this is the death of the king and they are all peculiar to Matthew's Gospel.

We do not read of the rent vail in John's Gospel. In fact, John omits many things. The Lord speaks of His ascension in John but there is no record of it, indicating that the one who is the Son of God does not need to ascend as He is the One who fills the whole universe. Again, when we have brought before us, uniquely in John's Gospel, the worship of this day in which we live, the emphasis is that it is not at Jerusalem nor at mount Gerizim but worship is in the spirit anywhere and at anytime. Against that background, the rending of the vail would not suit John's Gospel.

In the Gospels the vail was rent in twain from top to bottom and it is important to observe that in Matthew and Mark the rending of the vail has the thought not that man is now able to enter through a rent vail but that God is coming out. The vail was not removed, withdrawn or rolled up but rent and, notice, this rending occurred the moment He died; even before His body was taken down from the cross the vail was rent.

The words of Hebrews chapter 10 are important to understand in this connection. 'Having therefore, brethren, boldness to enter into the holiest by the blood of Jesus, by a new and living way, which he hath consecrated for us, through the veil, that is to say, his flesh; and *having* an high priest over the house of God; let us draw near with a true heart in full assurance of faith, having our hearts sprinkled from an evil conscience, and our bodies washed with pure water', Heb. 10. 19-22.

What a privilege belongs to us in this day! God, who formerly shut Himself in and man out, now says 'I want you to enter' and 'I want you to draw near'. Indeed, He says, 'enter with boldness' and 'draw near with full assurance'. In Hebrews chapter 10, the vail is neither removed nor rent for this is not God coming out but we entering and drawing near. God has come out without reserve, as seen in the rent vail, but we cannot enter without reserve. We enter not through the rent vail but through the vail, which is still there as far as our entry is concerned.

Hebrews chapter 10 is not commonly understood as it should be. Sometimes people speak of 'the rent vail of our redeemer's flesh' but I do not think that is the teaching of the passage. There were two things, self and sin, which kept man out from God's presence. Self is what I am in my Adam standing; sin relates to that which has been committed but, praise God, both of these things have been dealt with. One was dealt with in His blood and the other was dealt with in His flesh. 'By the blood of Jesus' tells me that the blood has dealt with my sin. That gives me boldness, (lit. 'frank speaking'), to enter. 'By a new a living way . . . that is to say His flesh' refers to His flesh given in death. When it is His flesh given, that is the termination of my Adam standing. There was removed before God in the death of Christ (that is, in His flesh given in death) the order of man Christ represented on the cross. Thus, not only has my sin been removed but also myself, in my Adamic standing, has been removed and now I enter through the vail.

The expression, 'that is to say His flesh' does not qualify 'the vail' but the 'new and living way'. The expression 'flesh' is scarcely used in relation to our Lord's person but rather in relation to His death. For instance, 'The bread that I will give is my flesh, which I will give for the life of the world', John 6. 51.

'And you, that were sometime alienated and enemies in *your* mind by wicked works, yet now hath he reconciled in the body of his flesh through death, to present you holy and unblameable and unreproveable in his sight', Col. 1. 21-22.

There is no thought of priesthood as distinct from laity today. This right and privilege to enter the holiest belongs to those who are 'brethren', all who are Christ's. How wonderful to think that we enter through the vail by a newly slain way! This indicates that the sacrifice of Calvary is as efficacious for us today as if it had just taken place this morning. It is also a living way. What is in view in this expression is not that the One who died now lives; rather, it reminds us that if an Israelite had entered the holiest of all he would have died but we are able to enter at all times. For us, it is a living way; there is no threat of death for us.

We also draw near, 'having our hearts sprinkled from an evil conscience, and our bodies washed with pure water'. Undoubtedly, the reference is to the consecration of the priests of old, when their bodies were washed by Moses and they themselves were sprinkled by blood. In this our attention is again directed to Calvary and the fact that 'forthwith came there out blood and water' from our Saviour's pierced side. It is Calvary that gives us the authority to enter the holiest in this present day. The reference is not, of course, to our baptism. After all, it was not the literal physical heart that was sprinkled with blood and so it is not the literal, physical body that was washed.

Washing by water and washing by blood is different. Washing by blood is judicial cleansing, connected with sins, but washing by water is moral cleansing, connected with the old nature. 'Our hearts sprinkled' with blood has to do with the question of our guilt; the sprinkled blood sets me free from the evil conscience that would continue to accuse me of my past guilt, the sins I have committed. 'Our bodies washed with pure water' has to do with our new birth and involves the new life that is suited to such an environment; we are born of water and of the Spirit. Both of these, the sprinkling and the washing, give us, today, the right of entry into the holiest, the immediate presence of God.

A question might be raised regarding the significance of the sprinkling of the people and the book by blood in Exodus chapter 24. The idea was that for disobedience there must be the death of either the people or the sacrifice. This links with the 'sprinkling of the blood of Jesus Christ', 1 Pet. 1. 2; we, too, have been sprinkled with blood and this indicates that all our disobedience has been completely met in the blood of such a sacrifice as was offered at Calvary.

The Ark and the Mercy Seat
Exodus 25. 10-22; 25. 17-22

The ark

The word 'ark' simply means a chest. The ark is, in fact, the most important of all the vessels of the tabernacle. Indeed, both the tabernacle and the temple were erected for the ark. The ark, with its mercy-seat, as we shall see later, provided God with His throne, where He would dwell and from whence He would speak to Moses. Not only did God dwell between the cherubim, when the tabernacle was erected and speak to Moses from between the cherubim from off the mercy-seat but, in Numbers chapter 10, it went first in the journey through the wilderness to seek out a place for the children of Israel. This was because of Moses' failure in relation to Hobab.

The ark is the first vessel that is mentioned in the details of the tabernacle after God has said, 'Let them make me a sanctuary', Exod. 25. 8. Later, David accorded it the first place and Solomon had it carried into the most holy of the temple. In fact, the ark is the only vessel of the tabernacle that was taken into Solomon's temple.

The ark is the only vessel that had a history apart from the tabernacle. Not only did it have its place in the holiest but it was, for instance, carried through Jordan, around Jericho, and into the battlefield. It was placed alongside the god in the house of Dagon and it was for a while in the house of Obed-edom.

Its sacredness can be understood by reason of the recurring mention of coverings. We have already seen that the vail was a covering vail as it covered the ark with the mercy seat. Also, the mercy seat covered the ark. In Exodus chapter 25 verse 20, we are told that the cherubim covered the mercy seat. Additionally, the Shekinah covered the mercy seat and, on the Day of Atonement, incense covered the Shekinah. All this covering speaks of the sacredness of the vessel.

The ark had a multitude of designations. It is called the 'ark of the testimony', the 'ark of the covenant', the 'ark of God', the 'ark of His strength', the 'holy ark', the 'ark of the Lord God of all the earth', and so on.

Its position

'And thou shalt put the mercy seat upon the ark of the testimony in the most holy *place*', 26. 34. The ark had its place within the vail in the Holy of Holies.

Its material

The ark was made of shittim wood overlaid within and without with pure gold, 25. 10-11.

Its dimensions

'Two cubits and a half shall be the length thereof, and a cubit and a half the breadth thereof, and a cubit and a half the height thereof', 25. 10.

Its design

There was a crown of gold round about the ark, 25. 11, and it had four rings of gold, v. 12. It had staves of shittim wood overlaid with gold, v. 13, that the ark may be borne with them, v. 14. These staves were to be in the rings of the ark and were not to be taken from it, v. 15, although they were removed at a later time when it was taken into the temple. There were, of course, certain instances when these staves were abused, when the ark was carried where it ought not to have been carried.

Its contents

'And thou shalt put into the ark the testimony which I shall give thee', 25. 16. The ark contained the two unbroken tables of the covenant, the unbroken tables of 'the ten words'. In addition, it contained 'the golden pot that had manna', Heb. 9. 4, and the same verse tells us that in the ark there was also 'Aaron's rod that budded'.

Moses went up twice into the mount. On the first time he came down with the tables of the law which, because of the worship of the golden calf, were broken. Then, Moses went up again and it is remarkable that he was there for two periods of forty days. He was forty days in intercession and a further forty days to receive another two tables of the covenant. This time God told him that because the first had been broken he had to make an ark of shittim wood into which these tables had to be put so that they might not be broken. I believe that this is, in fact, the same ark, but now in the holiest it is overlaid within and without with gold. I would suggest that the ark of shittim wood in Deuteronomy chapter 10 speaks of Christ as a man down here who 'magnified the law and made it honourable', Isa. 42. 21. He said, 'Thy law *is* within my heart', Ps. 40. 8. In Exodus 25, however, the law is in the ark that is made of shittim wood overlaid with pure gold and this would speak of that man glorified in Godhead glory. The unbroken tables of the covenant in the ark would be a reminder of the people's failure as outside of that ark the tables had been broken. However, if in the hands of men these tables were broken, they are secure in one who sits at God's right hand in heaven.

Initially, the two tables of stone were all that was in the ark, which is why it was called the ark of the *testimony* or the ark of the *covenant*. It was subsequent to the people receiving the manna and their failure to keep the instructions with regard to it that manna had to be laid up before the testimony to be kept, Exod. 16. 33. In Exodus chapter 16 two statements are used in connection with the manna. First of all, it lay upon the face of the wilderness, v. 14, and, secondly, it was laid up before the testimony, before the Lord, v. 34. Hebrews chapter 9 throws light on the statement that it was laid up before the Lord to be kept by indicating that it was put into a golden pot. The manna that lay on the face of the wilderness is Christ here in humiliation but the manna laid up before the Lord in this golden pot is Christ in His exaltation. The same manna that was here is now there; He has carried His manhood back to heaven, His kinship back to the throne of God. Thus, I suggest, the manna in this golden pot speaks of a Man now enshrined in Godhead glory. In that day, when we shall behold His glory, John 17. 24, we shall see a Man in heaven enshrined in Godhead glory.

It was after another failure, the rebellion of Korah, Dathan and Abiram in Numbers chapter 16, that Aaron's rod that budded found its place in the ark. That rod relates to God's vindication of the priesthood; a dead rod budding speaking of a priest on the other side of death.

When the ark was brought into the temple the golden pot that had manna and Aaron's rod that budded were not there, because that temple speaks of the future millennial glory. However, the whole background to the Epistle to the Hebrews is not the temple but the tabernacle of testimony in the wilderness; that is why they're mentioned in that letter.

The mercy seat

Its position

The mercy seat was, in fact, the lid of the ark. 'Thou shalt put the mercy seat above upon the ark', Exod. 25. 21. The crown was on the top of the ark and the mercy seat would rest securely between the surrounding crowns.

Its dimensions

Its length was two and a half cubits and its breadth was one and a half cubits, v. 17. No measurement is given as to its height.

Its design

On the two ends of the mercy seat there were two cherubim of gold of beaten work, v. 18-19.

Its material

The mercy seat, or the propitiatory, comes from a verb which means 'to cover'. It was made of pure gold, v. 17. We learn from Leviticus chapter 16 that blood was sprinkled upon it. In connection with the mercy-seat, the thought is not that of pure gold and wood but pure gold and sprinkled blood. God does not dwell among us on account of our Saviour's incarnation but on the ground of blood that has been shed, by one who is no less a person than the Son of God Himself.

God dwelt between the cherubim. Hezekiah addressed God in prayer as the 'Lord God of Israel, which dwellest *between* the cherubims', 2 Kgs. 19. 15. Psalm 8 verse 1 says, 'Thou that dwellest *between* the cherubims, shine forth'. 'He sitteth between the cherubims' is the language of Psalm 99 verse 1. Not only did He dwell there but from between the cherubim He spoke, as He met and communed with Moses. The ground on which the Lord was able to dwell in the midst of His people and speak to Moses was sprinkled blood. Inside the ark were the unbroken tables of the covenant, a covenant that they could not keep even though three times they said that all that the Lord had spoken they would do. These unbroken tables of the covenant must be covered and blood be sprinkled upon the covering, so that the cherubim looking down on the blood upon that pure gold saw that divine justice had been satisfied. It was only when the blood was sprinkled on it, therefore, that it became a mercy seat.

There was an instance when the men of Beth-shemesh took the lid off the ark and looked into it, with the result that fifty thousand and seventy of them were slain. Quite often this is interpreted as indicating that it is possible to be too inquisitive as to the person of Christ, looking into the truth of His person beyond that which we are expected to do. I suggest, however, that is not the reason why the men of Beth-shemesh were slain; rather, it is because once they took the lid off the ark and looked in they were brought face to face with the unbroken tables of the covenant. No mortal man can be brought face to face with the unbroken tables of the covenant and live; they must smite him. Now, God was to dwell with His people and the conditions were that they must cover the tables of the covenant with the mercy seat and blood must be shed and sprinkled upon it. This indicated that divine justice had been satisfied in respect of the claims of the law against His people and on that ground He would dwell among them.

'The cherubims shall stretch forth their wings on high, covering the mercy seat with their wings, and their faces shall look one to another; toward the mercy seat shall the faces of the cherubims be', Exod. 25. 20. Their wings are outstretched in order to cover the mercy seat. Instead of flying to execute judgement, these wings are covering the mercy seat, with their faces one toward another toward the mercy-seat. Their faces have a common object; they are bowed and gazing upon the blood, upon the pure gold. The first mention of cherubim is Genesis chapter 3 when, after sin entered, man was driven out and there was placed at the east of the garden cherubim and a flaming sword. However, the cherubim seen in connection with the mercy seat have no flaming sword; it has been sheathed in the sacrifice on the altar whose blood has been carried in and sprinkled on the pure gold. These cherubim are gazing upon blood upon the pure gold of God's throne. That is the ground on which God can meet with us too and dwell in our midst today.

The Day of Atonement

On the Day of Atonement, the tenth day of the seventh month, the priest entered through the vail and did so three times. First of all, he entered with the censer, with the live coals therein and the incense. He burned the incense upon the live coals on his first entry in order that that incense might cover the shekinah, the glory that was above the mercy seat. This was because as a mere mortal man Aaron could not have stood face to face before the glory of God and remained alive. He could only go in when the glory was enveloped and he was, of course, covered in the incense that speaks of Christ.

Then, he came out and the bullock was killed for the sins of the priestly family. He came in the second time with that blood, sprinkled it once on the throne and seven times before it. Blood sprinkled once on the throne was for the eye of God and seven times before the throne is for the meeting of man's need. In the New Testament the blood is mentioned in connection with meeting the seven-fold need of man and every issue that sin brought in its train as far as man is concerned was fully met by that precious blood. On that ground, the priestly family had their sins taken away.

The priest sprinkled the blood with his finger. When he went in the first time his hands were filled with the incense but in connection with the blood it is only his finger that is mentioned. The incense speaks of His person whereas the blood speaks of His work; and His person is always greater than His work.

Then, he came out and a goat was killed. The blood of that goat, which was for the sins of the people, was then taken in by the priest. He sprinkled it on and before the throne as he did in the first instance. The nation did not know they were forgiven until the high priest appeared again. At this point, he placed his hand upon the live goat, the scapegoat, and confessed over it the sins, iniquities and transgressions of the people. Obviously, he could not name each one of them and I think the confession was in the simple act of laying his hand upon the head of the scapegoat. The scapegoat was then let go into a land uninhabited, led by the hand of a fit man, and it was only then that the nation knew their sins had been forgiven.

This has meaning for us today. In Hebrews chapter 9 there are three appearings of our Lord. 'Once in the end of the world hath he appeared to put away sin by the sacrifice of himself', v. 26, speaks of the animal slain at the altar. Secondly, 'Christ is not entered into the holy places made with hands, *which are* the figures of the true; but into heaven itself, now to appear in the presence of God for us', v. 24, speaks of His first entry with blood for the priestly family, a family that speaks of us. Christ is now before the face of God in all the value of His shed blood for us and the fact that we know that He is there on our behalf gives us the enjoyment of our sins having been taken away. The third appearing, 'unto them that look for him shall he appear the second time without sin unto salvation', v. 28, is His future appearing for the nation of Israel. Notice the change in language: in verse 24 He now appears in the presence of God *'for us',* but this third appearing is *'unto them'* that look for Him, speaking of His having gone in and sprinkled the blood and His appearing in relation to the nation of Israel. They shall then look upon Him whom they have pierced and He will make good to them the benefits and blessings of Calvary.

Propitiation

In the New Testament there is brought before us the great truth of propitiation. It is mentioned in 1 John chapters 2 and 4, Hebrews chapter 2 and Romans chapter 3.

John tells us of the *person* who is the propitiation. 'He is the propitiation for our sins: and not for ours only, but also for *the sins of* the whole world', 1 John 2. 2. 'Herein is love, not that we loved God, but that he loved us, and sent his Son *to be* the propitiation for our sins', 4. 10.

Hebrews speaks of the *work* of propitiation. 'Wherefore in all things it behoved him to be made like unto *his* brethren, that he might be a merciful and faithful high priest in things *pertaining* to God, to make reconciliation (propitiation) for the sins of the people', Heb. 2. 17.

Romans speaks of the *place* of propitiation, the propitiatory, the mercy seat, when Paul writes, 'Whom God hath set forth *to be* a propitiation through faith in his blood', Rom. 3. 25. Thus, Christ is the person, He did the work, and He is the place of propitiation.

There is certainly no thought in God's word of a 'limited atonement'. If we say that the propitiation that He made only extends to the elect then we are limiting the power of the blood. In fact, not only did He make propitiation but, John says, 'He is the propitiation'. This relates to His person and a limited atonement would therefore impinge on the value of His own person. Let us remember, too, that He shed His blood when He 'gave Himself a ransom for all', 1 Tim. 2. 6, and if what He gave only sufficed for so many, then there was a limited ability on His part to save; this is because if He gave Himself, and if He shed His blood then He could have given no more. These are really important matters. Peter says it is 'precious blood' in the same chapter in which he speaks of God's son as God's 'elect and precious'. The precious Christ of God and the precious blood of Christ are found in the same chapter. Christ has invested His own blood with the preciousness of His own blessed person.

Some say that when Hebrews chapter 2 verse 17 speaks of Him making 'propitiation for the sins of the people' it relates to the sins only of His people, but the reason for this is that, in the context, the writer is only speaking of the people. The passage speaks of 'the seed of Abraham', 'His brethren' and 'the people'. In Galatians chapter 2, Paul speaks of 'the Son of God who loved me, and gave Himself for me', but Paul did not mean that the Son of God only gave Himself for him! Again, in Ephesians chapter 5, Paul says that 'Christ loved the church and gave Himself for it' but this does not mean that He gave Himself only for the church; in fact, He 'tasted death for every man', or 'every thing', Heb. 2. 9. In a coming day, the curse will be removed from the whole earth because of Calvary and this underlines that His was an *infinite* sacrifice, and of infinite value.

The staves of the ark

It is interesting to observe that the ark was the only vessel that was covered externally with blue and it would therefore be the most conspicuous of all the vessels as the people marched through the wilderness. I sometimes link that with the word that Mark says of our Lord Jesus Christ, 'He could not be hid', Mark 7. 24. This heavenly Man could not be hid.

Numbers tells us that the ark was to be carried on the shoulders of the Kohathites, but there were three occasions when it was carried on the shoulders of the priests. The priests carried the ark through the Jordan, round Jericho and, finally, into the oracle in the temple.

The staves never had to be drawn out. The ark continually journeyed with them and reminds us of the One who said, 'Lo, I am with you alway'. We can always be assured of His presence with us. At last it was taken into the temple and the staves were withdrawn, indicating that we shall be assured of His presence day by day until at last we are in His presence.

THE BURNT OFFERING
Leviticus 1

The book of Exodus begins with a groaning people; the book of Leviticus begins with a worshipping people. The word of God to Moses at the burning bush was, 'I have surely seen the affliction of my people which are in Egypt, and have heard their cry by reason of their taskmasters; for I know their sorrows', Exod. 3. 7. The children of Israel were down in Egypt groaning and their groans ascended to the God of heaven. In the book of Leviticus, however, the children of Israel have become a worshipping people for, in chapter 1, the Israelite is seen to be standing near to the brazen altar, his burnt offering ascending to God as worship, as a sweet savour. The change has been brought about by the fact that they are now a redeemed people. The divine intent with respect to the children of Israel had now been achieved. God had said, 'Israel is my son, even my firstborn' and 'Let my son go, that he may serve me', or 'religiously serve or worship me'. God had said to Moses, 'And let them make me a sanctuary; that I may dwell among them', Exod. 25. 8, and so now God has His redeemed people around Him in the wilderness; He is dwelling in their midst and they have become a worshipping people.

One of the key expressions of the book of Leviticus is, 'And He called'. In fact, the title of the book in the King James Version of Leviticus is really the title of the book in the Septuagint version, the Greek translation of the Hebrew scriptures. The title of the book in the original Hebrew is the word '*vayiqra*' which means 'and He called'. The title 'Leviticus' is somewhat misleading. It would lead us to think that here we have a book that is going to tell us about the Levites but it is the book of Numbers that does that. The book of Leviticus is the book that tells us about the priestly family and the title of the book in the original Hebrew, '*Vayiqra*', is certainly more appropriate because that word means, 'And He called'. In the book of Exodus God is heard to speak on a number of occasions. He spoke to Moses from the burning bush. He gave the law on Mount Sinai. He spoke to Moses face to face without the camp on the occasion of the apostasy of the nation of

Israel. In Leviticus, however, God is speaking not from a burning
bush, nor from Mount Sinai, nor from a place without the camp
but He is speaking from the mercy seat, His throne, in the midst
of His redeemed people. He has gathered them around Himself
and He speaks to Moses from the mercy seat. That mercy seat
was, of course, that golden lid that covered the ark. The
significance of that lid of gold, being God's throne and the mercy
seat, was that within the ark were the unbroken tables of stone.
The sons of Bethshemesh took the lid off the ark and peered into
it and because of that more than fifty thousand of them were slain.
Sometimes that has been interpreted that these men were more
curious than they might have been. That might be true but there
was more involved in the action than just that. Once they took the
lid off the Ark of the Covenant, they came face to face with an
unbroken law. For a sinner to come face to face with a unbroken
law cannot mean anything else but death, but God dwells in the
midst of His redeemed people. Once the unbroken tables of the
covenant had been covered with this lid of gold and it was
sprinkled with blood, then, on that basis, God dwelt in their midst
and from that throne He called to Moses. Each time we come
across the expression in Leviticus, 'And the Lord called', there
commences *a new and a different revelation of God Himself.*

Our Lord Jesus is presented in these offerings of Leviticus there.
John's presentation of the Son of God in his most interesting
Gospel is seen in the burnt offering. It is necessary to observe
John's omissions. For instance, when God's Son is in the garden
of Gethsemane in chapter 18 there is no mention of His sweat, of
His agony or of His being prostrate in the dust of the earth. In
fact, in John's Gospel it is those who have come to arrest Him
who are prostrate in the dust of the earth. There is no mention of
the angels sent from heaven to minister unto Him nor is there any
mention of the words of the Saviour, 'Father, if it be possible, let
this cup pass from me'. These are most important omissions. John
gives perhaps the most detailed account of the appearance of our
blessed Lord before Pilate. In His account of this it is possible to
begin, at first, to feel sorry for Pilate; he is quailing. Three times
over he is heard to protest that this man had done nothing worthy

of death and that he found no fault in Him. Pilate quails, not because of his wife's dream, nor because of her words, 'Have thou nothing to do with this just man', but because he discovers himself to be in the august presence of the Son of God.

There are important omissions in John's account of all that the Saviour endured on Golgotha's brow. He makes no mention of the prayer, 'Father forgive them, for they know not what they do'. He makes no mention of the pardon that the Son of God granted to the dying thief, the hours of darkness, nor the fact that God's Son was forsaken by God. He does not refer to the cry of the Saviour, 'My God, My God, why hast Thou forsaken me?' yet John was better able to give the details of Gethsemane and of Golgotha than was Matthew, Mark, or Luke. John, of course, was one of the favoured three who were with the Lord in the garden yet there are so many things that he does not mention. In addition, John was one of the faithful band of five who stood at the foot of the cross and because of that he was better equipped than the other evangelists to give the details of what happened at Golgotha. These omissions on John's part must be most important and the reason is that in John's Gospel God's Son is not presented as going into death to procure salvation or to put away sins. Rather, he presents God's Son going into death primarily for the glory of His Father; that in that death upon the cross He might bring eternal satisfaction and glory to His Father. This is an aspect of the death of Christ that is all too often forgotten. It is possible to be so selfish that whenever we think of Calvary we think only in terms of the blessing that it has brought but John tells of all the glory that Calvary brought to God the Father.

The Lord Jesus speaks of His death in the Gospel according to John in a particular way. In an amazing revelation He is heard to say, 'When ye have lifted up the Son of man, then shall ye know that I am', 8. 28. Again, the Saviour says, 'Now is my soul troubled; and what shall I say? Father, save me from this hour: but for this cause came I unto this hour', 12. 27. Then, He goes on to say, 'Father, glorify Thy name', v. 28. In effect, He says, 'Father I am going to Golgotha's brow and this is uppermost in my mind and heart that Thy name might be glorified'. Had there never been one soul saved, God's name had been eternally glorified by the death of His Son at the place called Calvary and it is from that standpoint that the sacrifice of the Saviour is viewed in the Gospel according to John. In John chapter 16, the Saviour says to His own, 'Behold, the hour cometh, yea, is now come, that ye shall be scattered, every man to his own, and shall leave me alone: and yet I am not alone, because the Father is with me'. From the beginning to the end of John's Gospel the Father is with His Son; hence, there is no mention of the abandonment, the hours of darkness and the orphan cry, 'Why hast Thou forsaken me?'

At the close of John chapter 14 the Saviour leaves the upper room with the words, 'That the world might know that I love the Father, arise, let us go hence'. Thus, in John's Gospel God's Son goes to Calvary that the world might know that He loved His Father.

In John chapter 10 the good Shepherd presents it from a different standpoint. There He is heard to say, 'Therefore doth my Father love me, because I lay down my life, that I might take it again', 10. 27. The Saviour went to Calvary in John's Gospel to show conclusively His love to the Father and in the consciousness of the Father's deep love to Him. In the upper room, once Judas had gone out and He begins to think of what lay before Him, He thinks of Calvary and is heard to say with regard to it, 'Therefore, when he was gone out, Jesus said, Now is the Son of man glorified, and God is glorified in him', 13. 31. At Calvary the Son of man was glorified in His perfect obedience and God was glorified in the sacrifice that He made. Accordingly, in John's Gospel we have the burnt offering aspect of the death of Christ in which God's Son goes into death neither to deal with sin nor, so much, to bring blessing to people but that the Father might be glorified. This brought eternal pleasure to the heart of His God and that is the burnt offering in John's Gospel.

The next offering is the meal offering of Leviticus chapter 2. The meal offering belongs to no one Gospel in particular; it can be seen in all of them. In the meal offering there is presented the holy life and the perfect service of the Son of man. Attention is directed to His wondrous person, His incorruptibility, His impeccable holiness and this, of course, belongs to no Gospel in particular. The meal offering is referred to as a 'memorial unto the Lord', indicating this important truth that the lovely life that He lived and the perfect service that He performed shall be a perpetual memorial to the heart of God.

The next offering in the book of Leviticus is the peace offering, in chapter 3. In the peace offering we have Luke's presentation of the life, service and death of the Lord Jesus Christ. In Luke chapter 7 there is the account of that woman of the city whose sins were forgiven and to whom the Saviour said, 'Go in peace', v. 50. Literally, the Saviour said not 'go *in* peace' but 'go *into* peace'. The significance of that is that, following the moral order of Luke's Gospel, she would go into the company that is spoken of in the opening verses of chapter 8, into the peace of the fellowship of that company of women who were following Christ and ministering to Him of their substance. This is the idea of the peace offering.

Furthermore, the peace offering was a thanksgiving offering. It is spoken of in Leviticus chapter 7 as the sacrifice of thanksgiving and throughout Luke's Gospel there is repeatedly the idea of thanksgiving, worship and praise. In Luke chapter 2 we read of the shepherds that they 'returned, glorifying and praising God for all the things that they had heard and seen, as it was told unto them', v. 20. In the same chapter the angels glorify God saying, 'Glory to God in the highest', v. 14. Here is a note of glorification, of gratitude and of worship. Again, in chapter 4, the Lord Jesus is in the synagogue where He taught, 'being glorified of all', v. 15. God is being glorified in chapter 2 and His Son is being glorified in chapter 4. Then, in chapter 5, there is the man with the palsy whose sins were forgiven. When the Lord Jesus said to him, 'Arise, and take up thy couch, and go into thine house', v. 24, he departed to his own house carrying his bed and glorifying God. In chapter 7, the Lord raises to life the son of the widow of Nain with the result that 'there came a fear on all: and they glorified God, saying, that a great prophet is risen up among us; and, That God hath visited his people', v. 16. In chapter 13 is the woman who was bound eighteen years. The Lord Jesus made her straight immediately and her reaction was that she began to glorify God. Chapter 17 contains the account of the ten lepers that were cleansed; one Samaritan leper returned and with a loud voice glorified God. In chapter 18 there is the blind man who received his sight and after he had received his sight he followed Him glorifying God and the people also gave praise to God. In chapter 23 the centurion at the foot of the cross, when he saw what was done, 'glorified God, saying, Certainly this was a righteous man', v. 47. Again, in chapter 19 the Lord Jesus enters Jerusalem and the whole multitude of the disciples are rejoicing and praising God with a loud voice. The Pharisees approached Jesus and said, 'rebuke thy disciples', v. 39. Jesus replied, 'I tell you that, if these should hold their peace, the stones would immediately cry out'. Here, then, is the peace offering. In Luke's presentation of the Saviour there is a sacrifice of thanksgiving and the theme from beginning to end is one of praise and of glorifying God.

The next offering is the sin offering in chapter 4, followed, in chapters 5 and 6, by the trespass offering. There is a difference between the sin offering and the trespass offering. In the sin offering there is mention made of the various persons who might sin but we are not told the type of sin that they might commit save that it is against the commandments of the Lord. There are no details of the sins as the emphasis is on the persons who might sin. In the trespass offering, however, no mention is made of the individual who might sin as the emphasis is rather on the type of sin or trespass they might commit. An Israelite might tell his neighbour a lie or deceive his neighbour in a matter of fellowship or there might be something that he has taken by violence; details are given about the different types of trespass.

In Mark's Gospel there is the sin offering but in Matthew's Gospel the trespass offering. What makes this clear is the words of the Lord Jesus on the occasion of His giving thanks for the cup at the institution of the Lord's Supper. In Mark's Gospel He is heard to say, 'This is my blood of the new testament, which is shed for many', 14. 24. That answers to the sin offering; His blood was shed for the persons. In Matthew's Gospel the words of the Lord Jesus are somewhat different. He says, 'This is my blood of the new testament, which is shed for many for the remission of sins', 26. 28. It is for the remission of sins and answers to the trespass offering.

The Lord Jesus is seen in a very special way in the burnt offering. The burnt offering was not offered because of any sin that had been committed. Rather, it gives us to appreciate the God-ward aspect of the death of Christ; not a death for sin but a death that might bring eternal glory to the heart of God. There is, of course, in connection with the burnt offering the idea of atonement. It is mentioned in chapter 1 verse 4, where we read, 'And he shall put his hand upon the head of the burnt offering; and it shall be accepted for him to make atonement for him'. In this matter of atonement there is the God-ward aspect, seen in the burnt offering, and the man-ward aspect of it, seen in the sin offering. The idea of atonement in the burnt offering is that of our acceptance but in the sin offering it is rather a different aspect of atonement. Chapter 4 verses 20, 26 and 35 say this, 'And the priest shall make an atonement for him' and his sin was forgiven. Notice the difference: in the burnt offering it is atonement with a view to acceptance whereas in the sin offering it is atonement with a view to forgiveness.

In both the burnt offering and the sin offering the offerer placed his hand upon the head of the offering but the hands that were placed on the head of the burnt offering were different in character from the hands that were placed on the head of the sin offering. The hands that were placed on the head of the burnt offering were worshipping hands, but those that were placed on the head of the sin offering were guilty hands, hands that had just sinned. When the hand was placed on the head of the burnt offering, it was the thought of identification, but when the hand was placed on the head of the sin offering it was the thought of transference of guilt.

The Israelite brought his burnt offering. He placed his hands upon its head and then saw it cut into its pieces and laid in order upon the altar, the head, the legs, and the inwards. He then saw it all ascending to God as a sweet incense, as an odour of a sweet smell into the nostrils of the God of heaven. As he saw it ascending, he realized that he had been accepted in the offering with which he had become identified in all the sweet odour of that offering to God. In the sin offering, however, the priest, once he had sinned, laid his guilty hands upon the head of that sin offering. He saw that offering, the head, the legs, the skin, the flesh, and the dung carried outside the camp and, in the place where the ashes were poured out, he saw that head upon which he had confessed sin reduced to ashes and put away out of his sight and out of the sight of God. He knew that then his sins were forgiven. In the burnt offering the emphasis is on what went up, but in the sin offering it is on what has been put away. It is atonement in its God-ward aspect that gives us acceptance in the burnt offering; it is atonement in its man-ward aspect that gives us to enjoy forgiveness in the sin offering.

You will notice in connection with the burnt offering that there was laid on the altar for God, in accordance with verses 8 and 9, the head, the legs and the inwards of the animal. I suggest that the *head* directs our attention to what Paul had to say with regard to God's Son. Paul says, 'He knew no sin'. The *legs* have to do with Peter saying of God's Son, 'He did no sin'. The *inwards* have to do with what John said of God's Son, 'And in Him is no sin'. In verses 9 and 13, before the legs and the inwards were placed on the altar, they had to be washed that they might become typically what Christ was intrinsically.

In connection with the offering of the birds in the burnt offering, according to verse 17, they had to be cleaved, but not divided.

This was always true in connection with the offering of birds in the Old Testament. I wonder why. I am told by those who know better than me that you could not divide a bird without breaking a bone. How beautifully accurate is the word of God! 'A bone of him shall not be broken', John 19. 36.

In connection with the offering of the birds in verse 16, the crop and the feathers had to be taken away and cast beside the altar on the east part by the place of the ashes. In the margin of the Bible there is a slight alteration here. It reads, 'He shall pluck away his crop with his filth' rather than with the 'feathers'. Both the crop and the filth of the birds had to be taken away. The crop is that part in the bird where it stores its undigested food. The crop had to be taken away and in this is represented our appreciation of God's Son. Frequently, this act of taking away the crop is presented as being the work of the priest but this was in fact the work of the offerer. When the priest was to do anything it was carefully stated that the priest was to do it but when it was the offerer that was to do something it is carefully stated that it was he who did it. Verse 15 provides that the priest shall bring it unto the altar and wring off his head and burn it on the altar. In verse 16 'he', that is the offerer, shall pluck away his crop with his feathers. In verse 17, 'he' shall cleave it with the wings. Then it says, 'And the priest shall burn it'. When it is 'he' it is the offerer; when it is the priest it is precisely stated that it was the priest. It was not the work of the priest to take away the crop and the filth, that was the work of the offerer. Oftentimes this is taken to refer to the work of our great High Priest in the sanctuary which God built and not men, in that He takes away from our worship everything that is not acceptable to God but I suggest that what we have here is not the work of the priest but the responsibility of the offerer. The offerer was to take away the crop and this relates not so much to the person of Christ but our appreciation of Him. We may learn that God finds no pleasure when we offer to Him what we have never digested. The saints are usually aware when a brother is offering in his worship what he has never made his own. It is so easy to acquire a big library and, if one is a good reader, to absorb what is written in books yet never to make it one's own. God does not really want what has never been digested, what has not been made one's own. I remember listening to a brother ministering in my home town many years ago when I was but a lad and coming down the road after the meeting I said to an Irish brother, 'Well, what did you think of that ministry today?' 'Ah', he said, 'he just succeeded in being nobody; he was neither himself nor the man who wrote the book'. God wants us to be ourselves and God wants us to offer to Him what we've made our own; what we have fed upon and digested.

He was not only to take away the crop but also the filth, the residue of what has been digested. In other words, if God does not want what we have not digested, God also wants freshness. Take away the filth. It is true that it is possible that there is offered to God Lord's Day by Lord's Day the same old thing. It is sad when the saints really know the next thing that is going to be said because it has been said for years. God wants freshness in our worship. Take away what has not been digested; take away everything that is not fresh.

In connection with the burnt offering there could be offered a bullock, a sheep, a goat or birds. All of these speak of Christ. John presents the highest presentation of the glories of Christ in his Gospel. He tells us in his Epistle that in the family of God there are spiritual fathers, spiritual young men and spiritual infants and I suggest that the thought here is that the spiritual father offers a bullock, the spiritual young man offers a sheep or a goat and the spiritual infant offers a bird or birds. As account is taken of these three different offerings it is noticeable that there is depreciation in their value. Again, as the chapter proceeds, there is less discriminative detail in connection with the offerings. All of them were a sweet savour unto God and God found delight in them all, for they all spoke of Christ, but the great tragedy is that oftentimes those who ought to be spiritual fathers are but spiritual infants. I would encourage the young to go in for worship, for presenting to God your appreciation of His Son. We are not saved to serve, really, but we are saved to worship. 'Let my people go, that they may serve me in the wilderness', Exod. 7. 16. God wants from our hearts worship first of all; service then flows from that and when worship precedes service there is character according to God in that service we do for Him. 'Thou shalt worship the Lord thy God, and him only shalt thou serve', Luke 4. 8. If I read the scriptures for my own spiritual good and blessing there will be in my heart depth and real appreciation of the worth of God's Son. It is that which makes me a worshipper. Thus, I would encourage young believers to give worship that first place in your life and spiritual exercise and you will discover that there will be value and character added to what service you do for the Lord thereafter.

God's Son may be thought of in John's Gospel as the bullock, the sheep, the goat and the birds. This is very easy to observe. Connected with the bullock there is the thought of labour and of service. It is as if God said to the Israelitish farmer, 'If you are going to offer me a bullock I want the best of the herd'. In fact the language is 'the son of the herd'. Under the law, if he was to offer to God any of his herd, God would say, 'I want the best or none at all'. This means that if God would accept worship from an Israelite it must cost him something, reminding us of the language of David, 'Neither will I offer burnt offerings unto the Lord my God of that which doth cost me nothing', 2 Sam. 24. 24. God sets a value on His people's worship and wants from them that worship that costs them something. Mary's ointment was a pound of ointment of spikenard very costly and it is in the costly worship that God finds delight. The bullock conveys the thought of labour. 'Much increase is by the strength of the ox', Prov. 14. 4. The stronger the ox the greater the increase, for the ox was the Israelite's worker. In the Psalm which is a prayer for prosperity, Psalm 144, the prayer of the Israelite in verse 14 was, 'That our oxen may be strong to labour'. This is how John in his Gospel presents our blessed Saviour. 'My Father worketh hitherto, and I work', John 5. 17. 'I must work the works of him that sent me', John 9. 4. 'The works which the Father hath given me to finish, the same works that I do', John 5. 36. 'My meat is to do the will of him that sent me, and to finish his work', John 4. 34. In chapter 17 verse 4, He says to the Father, 'I have glorified thee on the earth: I have finished the work which thou gavest me to do'. In John's Gospel, therefore, God's Son is seen as God's tireless worker, the one who never left an unfinished work.

The thought connected with the sheep is, of course, not of work but of passive *submission*. The sheep can either be led or driven and this is found in John's Gospel. In chapter 18 verse 4, Jesus is in the garden and Judas with the soldiers and officers come to arrest Him with their lanterns, torches and weapons. Jesus said, 'Whom seek ye? They answered him, Jesus of Nazareth. Jesus saith unto them, I am'. The result was that they went backward and fell to the ground prostrate in the presence of the 'I am'. Then, the band, the captains and the officers of the Jews took Jesus and bound Him and led Him away. One moment they are awe stricken and prostrate on the ground in His presence and the next moment, as a submissive sheep, He submits to be bound and led away. In chapter 19 verse 10, Pilate says, 'I have power to crucify thee'. The Son of God said, 'Thou couldest have no power at all against me, except it were given thee from above'. Then, He submits to be taken and led away. He is truly the passive sheep.

If the offerer did not bring a sheep he could bring a goat. 'There be three things which go well, yea, four are comely in going: a lion which is strongest among beasts, and turneth not away for any; a greyhound; an he goat also; and a king, against whom there is no rising up', Prov. 30. 29-31. God's Son is the he-goat, comely in His going in John's Gospel. In John chapter 1 verse 29, John looking upon Jesus as He walked said, 'Behold the lamb of God'. In John chapter 7, Jesus walked in Galilee and, in chapter 10, He walked in Solomon's porch in the temple. In chapter 11, Jesus walked no more openly. There is a spiritual thought connected with every reference to the walk of Jesus in John's Gospel. He was comely in His going.

If the offerer could not bring a goat then he could offer birds. These depict the heavenly character of God's Son and this is what is presented in John's Gospel. 'I am not of this world', John 8. 23. 'He that cometh from above is above all', John 3. 31. In chapter 6 verse 50, He speaks of Himself as 'the bread which cometh down from heaven' and further says, 'I am the living bread which came down from heaven', John 6. 51. Here is the bird, heavenly in its character.

Doves or pigeons could be offered. Many thoughts are connected with the dove in God's word, one is that of mourning. In Isaiah chapter 38 verse 14, Hezekiah says, 'I did mourn as a dove'. 'We roar all like bears, and mourn sore like doves', Isa. 59. 11. It almost seems inappropriate in John's Gospel to have the Son of God mourning but in chapter 11, Jesus groaned in spirit. This is peculiar to John's Gospel; 'Jesus wept'.

Then the pigeon could also be offered. The outstanding feature of a pigeon is its homing instinct. In John's Gospel there is impressed upon our mind and heart the homing instinct of our blessed Saviour. We hear Him say in chapter 6 verse 62, 'What and if ye shall see the Son of man ascend up where he was before?' In John's Gospel the Son of God longs to go back to the place from whence He came. 'I came forth from the Father, and am come into the world: again, I leave the world, and go to the Father', John 16. 28. 'Father, the hour is come; glorify thy Son, that thy Son also may glorify thee', John 17. 1. It is the longing of the heart of God's Son to go back to the Father. In John chapter 1 verse 18, He is the only begotten Son which is in the bosom of the Father. This does not speak of His omnipresence but of the place where He now is. 'No man hath seen God at any time; the only begotten Son, which is in the bosom of the Father', (at the time of my writing) 'he hath declared him' (when He was here). The pigeon is back in the loft, back in the bosom of the Father from whence He had come. The Saviour would say as it were, 'This is not my home; I am just a stranger here'. The pigeon instinct is seen in this deep longing to go back to the place from whence He had come.

THE MEAL OFFERING

Leviticus 2

In the meal offering there is presented the perfect life and service of Jehovah's perfect Servant.

Outline

There are five different ways in which the meal offering might be offered.

In verses 1-3, the Israelite might take a handful of flour, of oil, of salt and all the frankincense and give it to the priest who would place it upon the altar that it might ascend as a sweet savour unto God. Then, in verses 4-7, there are three ways in which a cooked meal offering might be offered to the Lord. In verse 4, the Israelite might cook the meal offering in his tent and then bring it to the priest who in turn placed it upon the altar. Next, in verses 5-6, the Israelite might offer yet another kind of cooked offering, this time cooked in a pan; the word means a 'flat plate'. Thus, he might also cook it in a flat plate in his home and then bring that cooked offering to the priest who would in turn place it upon the altar. Then, in verse 7, it might be cooked in yet another way, this time in a frying pan. Having been cooked in a frying pan in the home, it would be taken to the priest who in turn would place it upon the altar. There are then four ways in which it could be offered; a handful uncooked, or a meal offering cooked in any of three ways (in an oven, on a flat plate or in a frying-pan) with the fifth mode of offering detailed from verse 14 to the end of the chapter. This time the Israelite might bring to the priest green ears of corn dried or parched by the fire, even corn beaten out of full ears. He would lay frankincense thereon and give it to the priest who in turn would place it upon the altar. It would ascend into the nostrils of God as a sweet savour. In a delightful way, all of this directs the heart to the person of our blessed, adorable Lord Jesus.

In verse 11, there are two prohibitions. God prohibited the offering of any leaven or any honey with a meal offering. Then, in verse 12, there is a prohibition in respect of the oblation of the firstfruits; they were to offer them unto the Lord but they must not burn them on the altar for a sweet savour. Chapter 23 indicates that the oblation of the firstfruits was the offering on the day of Pentecost when two wave loaves baked with leaven were waved to and fro before the Lord. Because of the presence of leaven in the oblation of firstfruits that oblation must not touch the altar.

Finally, in verse 13, we have a requirement. 'And every oblation of thy meat offering shalt thou season with salt; neither shalt thou suffer the salt of the covenant of thy God to be lacking from thy meat offering: with all thine offerings thou shalt offer salt'.

The component parts of the meal offering

The four component parts of the meal offering were flour, oil, salt, and frankincense. In God's word, when anything is described for us in a fourfold way, there is an invariable rule that three of the descriptions are similar and one is altogether different. Perhaps the obvious example is that of the four Gospels. The New Testament begins with the four Gospels, Matthew, Mark, Luke and John. The first three Gospels have been termed the 'synoptic Gospels' because of their striking similarity. In Matthew, Mark and Luke our blessed Lord is seen, so to speak, through the same eye but John's Gospel is altogether different and unique. Another example, in the Old Testament, occurs in connection with the manna, the corn of heaven which God rained down upon the children of Israel in the wilderness of Sin. That manna was described in Exodus chapter 16 in a fourfold way. It was small, round, white, and it tasted like cakes made with honey. The first three descriptions pertain to sight, how the manna looked, its appearance, but the fourth pertained to its taste. There is also a fourfold description given of Naaman the leper. He was great, honourable and mighty but the fourth description is that he was a leper. Also, in the Old Testament we have four different anointings. There was the anointing of the prophet, of the priest, and of the king but there was also that peculiar and altogether different anointing of the leper. We can understand how our Lord Jesus was anointed as prophet, priest, and king, but our Lord Jesus was, of course, never leprous in Himself in any way. However, He had a unique anointing when he was anointed in the house of Simon the leper, speaking of His identification with Israel in its leprous condition. There is, then, this invariable law in connection with anything described in a fourfold way that three descriptions are similar and the fourth is altogether different.

The unique component part of the four in connection with the meal offering is the frankincense and it is different in that the Israelite or the priest might partake of the flour, of the oil or of the salt, but not of the frankincense. All the frankincense must be laid on the altar for God; all the frankincense is His.

The **flour** directs attention to the holy manhood of our blessed Lord Jesus. This is a truth that is being assailed today but we need to establish in our minds that while the manhood of God's Son was perfect, His manhood was unique. There has been in this world three different kinds of manhood. Until sin entered, there was *innocent* manhood; since sin entered there has been *fallen* manhood; but when Mary brought forth her firstborn and swaddled Him, and laid Him in a manger, she introduced into this world a kind of manhood that the world had never seen before. It was not innocent manhood. It is true that Judas said, 'I have betrayed the innocent blood', Matt. 27. 4, but these are the words of Judas and not the words of inspiration. Of course, the Spirit of God inspired the writers to have these words included in the word of God but these words were not necessarily inspired and, in any case, Judas might have been thinking that at least Jesus was innocent of the charge that was laid against Him. The manhood of Jesus was not innocent manhood because innocent manhood is capable of sinning. Adam was created of God an innocent man; he was possessed of innocent manhood but he sinned. It is not that Jesus did not sin or that He would not sin but that He could not sin. His manhood was neither innocent nor fallen manhood.

Since sin entered into the world mankind has partaken of fallen manhood but God's Son never partook of fallen manhood. If He had He could never have been our Saviour. His was holy manhood. The angel said to Mary, 'That holy thing which shall be born of thee shall be called the Son of God', Luke 1. 35. The manhood of God's Son was impeccably *holy*.

This flour had to be fine flour. It had to be fine for it speaks to us of our Lord Jesus Christ. It seems to suggest that this had to be flour that was inherently fine rather than flour that had to be made fine through crushing. It was the finest of the flour. In that respect our blessed Lord Jesus differs from every other man or woman. Invariably, it is the case with His people that circumstances make them; the trials and difficulties of the journey help to produce features of Christ in them but circumstances never made Jesus. The trials of the pathway for God's Son never produced anything in Him. Every trial of the pathway only served to bring out the fineness that was inherently there.

The idea in fine flour is that its texture was even. It is wonderful to think of our blessed Lord Jesus in this respect. It has been beautifully pointed out that when we think of God's Son we never think of Him as being possessed of an outstanding characteristic, feature, virtue, or grace. Abraham was outstanding for his faith, Moses because of his meekness, John for his love and affection, but the Lord Jesus Christ is not to be thought of in that way for the simple reason that no one grace outshone another. If He had faith it was perfect; if meekness, it was perfect; if love, it was perfect; the texture was even.

There was also **oil**. The oil was applied in three different ways. In verses 4-5 there is a meal offering mingled with oil. In verse 4 there is a meal offering anointed with oil and then in verse 6 there is a meal offering broken in pieces and oil poured thereupon. The idea in the oil being poured thereon is that here there is a meal offering completely saturated with oil. All of this has an undoubted significance as oil in the scripture always speaks to us of the Holy Spirit of God. The Lord Jesus may be thought of, in relation to the Spirit, as a meal offering mingled, anointed and saturated with oil.

The meal offering *mingled with oil* directs our attention to His divine conception, the fact that He was conceived of the Holy Spirit of God. This is yet another of the precious truths in relation to the person of Christ that is being assailed today. Any man or woman who denies the virgin birth of Christ is not Christian. The virgin birth of Christ was essential because of His deity. If Christ was not virgin born He was just the child of Jewish peasants, born out of wedlock; being virgin born, He was conceived of the Holy Spirit of God. The first predictive utterance connected with our Saviour is when God says to the serpent, 'And I will put enmity between thee and the woman, and between thy seed and her seed; it shall bruise thy head, and thou shalt bruise his heel', Gen. 3. 15. He is truly the Son of Man but only the seed of the woman. Right down through the ages every godly mother in Israel trusted that she might be the mother of that promised one but none of them understood what was meant when it was said that that promised one must only be the seed of the woman. Mary did not understand it for when the angel said to Mary, 'Thou shalt conceive in thy womb, and bring forth a son', Luke 1. 31, Mary said, 'How shall this be, seeing I know not a man?' v. 34. The angel unfolded to Mary the wonderful secret, the amazing truth, of His divine conception, and explained to her that the Holy Spirit would come upon her for production and the power of the Highest would overshadow her for protection. That holy thing which would be born of her would be called the Son of God. There is the blessed fact and truth of His virgin birth; born of a woman yet conceived of the Holy Spirit of God. Scripture is not only eloquent with regard to what it says but with regard to what it does *not* say.

The idea of swaddling is only brought before us on three occasions in the Bible. It is in Job chapter 38, Ezekiel chapter 16 and Luke chapter 2. This affords a delightful study. Job speaks of the majesty of our blessed Lord that it was He who, when this world was but a vast watery waste, swaddled the deep in bands of dense darkness; but that same blessed one came down into this world, conceived of the Spirit of God, born of a woman and was Himself swaddled by that handmaid in Israel and laid in a manger. It is little wonder His people sometimes sing, 'Oh come let us adore Him!' as they consider His amazing condescension.

Ezekiel is given to appreciate the reason for Jerusalem's abomination which was that there had been failure in her nativity. When she was born she was neither cleansed, nor salted nor swaddled but was cast out into the open field to the loathing of her person. There had been serious omissions in her nativity but when God's Son was born into this world Mary swaddled Him and laid Him in a manger. There is no mention of cleansing but there is no omission as cleansing was completely unnecessary. He was born holy. Forthwith, He was swaddled with no need of cleansing. Later, in Luke chapter 2, Mary offers the birds for her cleansing but no mention is made of His cleansing; He was born holy. Here, then, is the meal offering mingled with oil.

In verse 4, there is the meal offering *anointed with oil*. It is not difficult to understand what is meant by the meal offering anointed with oil. The Lord Jesus, quoting from Isaiah in reference to His baptism, said, 'The Spirit of the Lord is upon me, because he hath anointed me to preach the Gospel to the poor', Luke 4. 18. His being anointed with the Spirit refers to being anointed with a view to service. This took place on the occasion of His baptism when, coming up out of the water, the Holy Spirit descended in bodily form as of a dove. It was then He was anointed. In John's presentation of that wonderful event he makes it clear that the one who came up out of the water was the Lamb of God. As He did so the Spirit descended like a dove and a voice that was heard from heaven was the voice of the Father, 'This is my beloved Son, in whom I am well pleased', Matt. 3. 17. All of this bespeaks complacency; a lamb, a dove and the voice of the Father.

Then, we have the offering *saturated with oil*. In verse 6, the meal offering was broken in pieces and oil poured on each several part. This speaks of the life of our Lord Jesus that from beginning to

144

end it was a life always under the complete control and guidance of the Holy Spirit of God. He was conceived of the Spirit of God, led of the Spirit of God into the wilderness, coming out of the wilderness in the power of the Spirit of God, casting out demons by the power of the Spirit of God, and, finally, offering Himself through the eternal Spirit without spot unto God. The meal offering saturated with oil speaks of a Man here under the control and guidance of the Holy Spirit of God.

The next component part is the **salt**. The salt speaks of His incorruptible holy nature. Salt is the great preservative and this speaks of the fact that our blessed Lord Jesus was possessed of an incorruptible and a holy nature. This 'must' of salt is seen against the two-fold prohibition, excluding honey and leaven. Honey is one extreme, leaven is another extreme, but salt is the great balancer. We may think of our Lord Jesus in this way. In Him there was no honey, and in Him there was no leaven but there was the salt, that which speaks of His incorruptible holy nature. When honey and leaven are brought together the idea is that honey speaks of sweetness and leaven of bitterness. (Honey does not always speak of human sweetness for there are occasions when it cannot refer to that. For instance, they gave to our risen Lord in Luke chapter 24 broiled fish and an honeycomb, and He partook of that and in it He found delight. Of course, scripture must be always studied in its context. We may think of them giving the Lord the honeycomb and the broiled fish in this way: honey is the product of industry and the fish are brought out of the deep. In connection with our worship this is that in which our Lord still finds delight. The great tragedy today is that so many of the Lord's people are not reading the scriptures and have therefore lost the art of being spiritually industrious in the things of God. Our Lord finds delight in that which is the product of spiritual industry and that which we can bring out of the deep by the help of the Spirit of God). Our Lord Jesus was never characterized by human sweetness nor was He affected by it. Peter says in Matthew's Gospel as the Lord Jesus had indicated He was going to Jerusalem, there to be killed, 'Be it far from thee, Lord: this shall not be unto thee', Matt. 16. 22. 'Pity thyself Lord'. The Lord

145

Jesus knowing that these were words of purely human sentiment and human sweetness replied, 'Get thee behind me, Satan: thou art an offence unto me: for thou savourest not the things that be of God, but those that be of men', v. 23. On His way to be crucified the daughters of Jerusalem follow Him wailing and lamenting. Well did the Lord Jesus know that the tears of these daughters of Jerusalem were tears of human sentiment and tears of pure emotion; they were certainly not tears of repentance. He said to them, 'Weep not for me, but weep for yourselves, and for your children', Luke 23. 28. In Him there was no honey nor was He ever affected by that which honey represents, human sweetness.

If there was no honey found in Him, neither was there leaven. If the honey speaks of human sweetness, the leaven speaks of human bitterness. This was absent from the Lord Jesus. In John chapter 2, when He purged the temple, He made a whip of small cords and drove out the oxen. He did not go amok as some would represent the Lord on that occasion in the temple. He said to those that sold the doves, 'Carry these things hence'. Human zeal would have degenerated into bitterness and would have gone amok, but not the Saviour. In Luke chapter 9 verse 54, He is approaching the villages of Samaria and they would not receive Him. The 'sons of thunder' said, 'Lord, wilt thou that we command fire to come down from heaven, and consume them, even as Elias did?' The Lord Jesus said, 'Ye know not what manner of spirit ye are of'. In Matthew chapter 14, there were gathered before Him 5000 hungry people. The disciples said, 'This is a desert place, and the time is now past; send the multitude away, that they may go into the villages, and buy themselves victuals', Matt. 14. 15. The Lord Jesus would not send them away, however, and He bade them sit down. He fed them with the loaves and fishes, but notice that He blessed the loaves and fishes and then He said to His disciples, 'Give them to eat'. That is not what others would have done. They would have said to the disciples, 'Now, you wanted to send them away, just you sit back and watch me feeding them', but the Lord Jesus graciously handed it to the disciples that they in turn might feed the hungry multitude. There is a lesson in this. All too often love and affection degenerates into pure sentiment and, on the other hand, anger which at first might be righteous all too easily degenerates into bitterness. The Lord Jesus was never characterized by these things. In Him there was no honey and no leaven.

God claimed **the frankincense** for Himself. While the Lord Jesus served men He was never the servant of men; He was the Servant of Jehovah. Everything that our Lord Jesus did was primarily for the pleasure and the satisfaction of Him whose servant He was. In Galatians chapter 1 verse 10, Paul says, 'Do I seek to please men? for if I yet pleased men, I should not be the servant of Christ'. He is stating that in his service he did not serve to please men but to please Christ. The moment the Christian begins to seek in service to please men is that moment the Christian ceases to be the servant of Christ. As Christ is served, His pleasure must be sought. Accordingly, while God's Son served men, He was never the servant of men in the sense of serving them to please them. Every service that He performed was primarily for the pleasure of the One whose Servant He was. 'Behold my servant, whom I uphold; mine elect, in whom my soul delighteth', Isa. 42. 1. He was God's Servant, whom God upheld; God's elect, the one in whom God's soul found delight because everything that He did was primarily for the pleasure of His God. God said, 'I want all the frankincense'.

The five modes of offering

There was first of all the *uncooked* handful; the handful of the flour, of the oil, of the salt with all the frankincense was placed on the altar and ascended as a sweet savour into the nostrils of God. This is suggestive of what occurs particularly at the Lord's Supper. We take our handful and, in a priestly way, we present it to God in worship. The hand speaks of capacity; the bigger the hand the greater the capacity. The bigger the hand of the Israelite the greater was the meal offering placed on the altar. Our prayer ought to be, 'O God, for bigger hands: O God, for a greater capacity to appreciate the wonders and the glories of Thine own Son'. It may be that our hands are small; our appreciation of

God's Son may be so very poor. Sometimes the Lord would have to say to us as He said to Philip, 'Have I been so long time with you, and yet hast thou not known me?' John 14. 9. It would please God should we go in for a deeper appreciation of His Son, that we might have a greater capacity to present Him in all His wondrous beauty to the heart of His Father. The meal offering uncooked may suggest what Christ is in Himself in His intrinsic worth, altogether apart from the circumstances of the pathway.

After the handful was placed on the altar, the remnant became the food of the priestly family and thus they actually fed on the same meal offering as had been placed on the altar. The handful was for God and the remnant for the priestly family. It is a tremendous truth that God has called His people into fellowship with Himself, to share with Him the pleasure and the delight that He has found in His own Son. Scripture is brim full of this line of teaching. On the occasion of our Lord's baptism God is heard to say, 'Thou art my beloved Son, in whom I am well pleased', Mark 1. 11. This directs attention to what He was to God, but on the occasion of His transfiguration the voice from the excellent glory employs different words and points to what God intends His Son to be to His people. He says, 'This is my beloved Son: hear him', Mark 9. 7. It is not then, 'Thou art' but 'This is'; not, 'In thee is all My delight' but 'Hear him'. In John chapter 6, He is the bread of God, that bread that has satisfied the heart of God, but He is also the bread that God has given to His people to eat; they feed on the same bread. In 1 Peter chapter 2 verse 4, He is God's elect and precious, but Peter also says, 'Unto you therefore which believe he is precious', v. 7. He is precious to God and God intends that He should be precious to us. God says, 'I want the handful and you can have what remains', as He desires that we share in all the pleasure that He has found in His own Son.

Next there was the *cooked* meal offering. There were different vessels, the oven, the flat plate and the frying-pan in which the meal offering might be cooked. While the meal offering was cooking in the oven it was completely enclosed and hidden from view. This refers not to Calvary, as it is sometimes presented, or to the hours of darkness, or to His abandonment, for, while Calvary might be involved in the meal offering, what is really emphasized is His holy life and service. The oven rather refers to the first thirty years of His life, about which so little is said in God's word, when He was growing up before God. This meal offering cooked in the oven could be cooked in two ways: it could be unleavened cakes of fine flour mingled with oil or unleavened wafers anointed with oil. Those thirty years of His life began as a meal offering mingled with oil, speaking of His Divine conception, and they ended with wafers anointed with oil, speaking of His being anointed for service. There is a difference to be noted here; unleavened cakes were mingled with oil but unleavened wafers were anointed with oil. The word for 'cakes' means 'thick cakes' whilst the word for 'wafers' is 'thin cakes'. Those thirty years began with thick cakes, representing His life as it was lived before God, but they ended with thin cakes, anointed, as He went out to serve God in the interests of men. There is a principle here: thick cakes God-ward and thin cakes man-ward indicate that He was always greater to God than He could ever be in the esteem of men. With us it may be oftentimes rather different. We can be such hypocrites, guilty of such false piety that we can appear in the eyes of our fellow men to be what we know we are not in the sight of God but this was never so in God's Son.

Then, verses 5 and 6, there is the meal offering cooked on a flat plate where, far from being hidden, it was altogether exposed to view. The Israelite and his family could watch the meal offering being cooked on this flat plate. The meal offering cooked on the flat plate speaks of His three and a half years of public service, seen and witnessed by men. It was this particular offering that was parted in pieces and oil poured on each several part. During the three and a half years of His public service, men parted Him in pieces as they analysed His every word and deed to find one flaw, one sin, one discrepancy. That they could never do. One day He stood before the Sanhedrin and He challenged these men, 'Which of you convinceth me of sin?' John 8. 46. If these men could have convicted our Lord Jesus of one sin they would have gladly done it. They scrutinized His every word and every deed; they ransacked His records to discover that in Him there was neither flaw, nor sin, nor discrepancy. Rather, here was a man who's every movement and every word was always under the control of the Holy Spirit of God. God has had many good servants who have served Him faithfully and well but God has had only one perfect Servant and here He is.

> No broken service Lord was Thine,
> No change was in Thy way;
> Unsullied in Thy holiness,
> Thy strength knew no decay.

In verse 7, the meal offering could be cooked in a *frying pan*. The frying pan differs from the oven and from the flat plate in that it is a vessel with walls. When the meal offering was cooking in the frying pan it was partly exposed and partly enclosed. This refers to the experience of God's Son in the garden of Gethsemane. The world never saw what happened there but heaven saw. There were legions of angels who were not only interested spectators but, at one word of His bidding, they would have come to His assistance.

Next, there is the meal offering of the first fruits, the *green ears of corn dried by the fire*, even corn beaten out of full ears. This refers to those forty days wherein God still found infinite pleasure and delight in this blessed Son between His resurrection and His being caught up. Green ears of corn parched by the fire undoubtedly refer to Calvary. Notice that it was green ears of corn that were parched by the fire, corn that is cut down while it is still green, before it has reached its maturity.

Before the flood, the man that lived longer than any other man was Methuselah, who lived for 969 years. After the flood, the man that lived the longest was Heber, and he lived for 464 years. After Babel, the man who lived the longest was Reu, who lived for 239 years. In the wilderness Psalm, 90, it indicates that the

150

days of our years are threescore and ten. Notice how man's years are continually being halved.

Our Lord Jesus was cut off in the midst of His days, Ps. 102. 24. When but thirty years and a little more, our Saviour was cut off at Calvary. It is a remarkable thing that although these ears were green they were full; it was corn beaten out of full ears. It is an unusual thing that they should be full before they've reached their maturity, reminding us of this tremendous truth that though God's Son was cut off in the midst of His days, while the ears were yet green, so to speak, there was a fullness in the life that eternity shall never all unfold. The life that He lived is going to be perpetually a memorial to the heart of our God. Though His was but a brief visit to this world in which we live, yet there was a fullness in that blessed life that eternity itself shall never, never, all unfold.

THE PEACE OFFERING

Leviticus 3; 7. 11-21, 28-34.

To arrive at a proper understanding of the significance of the peace offering, it is necessary to read both the account of the offering of the peace offering in Leviticus chapter 3 and the law of the peace offering in Leviticus chapter 7. From Leviticus chapter 1 verse 1 to chapter 6 verse 7, there are the offerings themselves and then, from verse 8 of chapter 6 to the end of chapter 7, there is the law pertaining to these offerings. The difference between the presentation of the offerings and the law of the offerings is that in the offerings themselves there is God's portion but in the law of the offerings we are directed to man's portion. The peace offering is that offering where everyone concerned in the sacrifice itself had a portion, and so it is necessary to read the law of the offering in chapter 7 in order to see the portion that each person had. In fact, I believe that that is why the peace offering has often not been properly understood; many have not taken time to observe the different parts of the sacrifice given to various individuals concerned in the offering of the sacrifice of the peace offering.

It is important to have established in our minds that in the peace offering the thought is not that of peace of conscience. This was not an offering that was offered in order to obtain peace; rather, it was an offering that was offered out of an *enjoyment of the peace of communion*. The word for 'peace' here is plural. This is most significant and indicates that here we have an offering that was offered to the Lord out of an enjoyment of peace in all its fullness and plenitude. The subject matter therefore is not peace of conscience but rather the peace of communion.

The peace offering was offered upon the burnt offering. 'And Aaron's sons shall burn it on the altar upon the burnt sacrifice, which is upon the wood that is on the fire', Lev. 3. 5. The fact that the peace offering was burned on top of the burnt offering must be underlined in the study of the peace offering. The thought in connection with the burnt offering is that of our acceptance before God. 'It shall be accepted for him to make atonement for him', 1. 4. As the Israelite stood beside the altar and saw the burnt offering that he had brought ascend as a sweet savour to God, he knew that he was accepted before Him in all the sweet savour of his burnt offering; it had been accepted for him. By way of contrast, in connection with the sin offering the emphasis is not on what went up as a sweet savour but what was put away from before the face of God, namely the offerer's sin. It is important to observe that the peace offering was not burned on the sin offering, but on top of the burnt offering. The significance is that we shall never know that fullness of peace that God intends we should enjoy if we never get any further than that our sins have all been forgiven. I arrive at that fullness of peace that God wants me to enjoy when I appreciate my acceptance before God, the fact that I am accepted in the beloved

Another important point to observe is that twice over in chapter 3, in verses 11 and 16, we are told that the peace offering was the food of the burnt offering. God thus commanded that all the internal fat, all the suet of the peace offering, had to be burned on the altar on top of the burnt offering. As the flame melted the suet of the peace offering it would flow over the burnt offering and increase the flame that was burning the burnt offering, causing the sweet savour to ascend all the more. One of the great differences between the burnt offering and the peace offering is that in the peace offering there is presented the dedication of God's Son to the will of God. The thought in the internal fat is of the inward excellence, the dedication of God's Son to the will of God, whereas in the burnt offering there is presented the vigour with which God's Son carried out the will of God. We learn, then, that the utter devotion and dedication of God's Son to the will of God was food and refreshment to His being and gave Him strength and vigour to carry it out. This can be seen in John chapter 4. The disciples had gone to obtain food. While they were absent Jesus was speaking with that woman of Samaria and when the disciples returned they marvelled that He spake with this woman. When she departed they said unto the Saviour, 'Master, eat'. He said, 'I have meat to eat that ye know not of'. It would almost appear that the disciples took another look at Jesus and, as they did so, it appeared as if Jesus had been refreshed. They said, 'Hath any given Him anything to eat?' The Lord Jesus said, 'My meat is to do the will of Him that sent me'; His dedication to God's will was food and refreshing to His being. This is something that many Christians need to learn today. Our dedication to the will of God can be food and refreshing to the whole being

In order to understand the significance of the peace offering we have to observe how the animal was apportioned and how each individual concerned in its offering had their particular portion. In Leviticus chapter 3, there is God's portion; in chapter 7, there is the portion of the officiating priest, the priestly family and the Israelite who brought the peace offering together with his family.

God's portion

We learn, in chapter 3 verse 3, that God claimed the fat that was upon the inwards. It was the suet of the animal that God claimed in the matter of the peace offering. Then, in verse 4, God claimed the kidneys of the animal and the caul above the liver. This is what has to be placed on the altar for God.

The fat was offered in connection with the burnt offering and the peace offering, but the word for fat is different in connection with each of these offerings. The fat of the burnt offering was the inner skin of fat of the animal, whereas the fat of the peace offering was the internal fat, the suet of the animal. We read in connection with the burnt offering that there was offered the head, and the legs, and the fat, the muscular fat, but in the peace offering no mention is made of the legs at all, only the internal fat. In the burnt offering it is the muscular fat which speaks of His vigour in service. The idea is that here in the peace offering our attention is directed to His inward excellence, the secret springs of the heart, His being utterly devoted to the will of God. In this, God found infinite pleasure. Little wonder God claimed the fat; only God could see this and therefore only God could appreciate it.

Then, God claimed *the kidneys*. The root meaning of the Hebrew word for 'kidneys' is 'to be perfect or complete'. This refers to the important principle that the Son of God completed every work to which He put His hand. He never left a task incomplete. Luke's Gospel is the gospel that presents to us the Lord Jesus Christ in the aspect of the peace offering, the one who finished every work to which He put His hand. In chapter 14, there is the parable uttered by the Lord peculiar to Luke's Gospel when He says, 'Which of you, intending to build a tower, sitteth not down first, and counteth the cost, whether he have sufficient to finish it? Lest haply, after he hath laid the foundation, and is not able to finish it, all that behold it begin to mock him', Luke 14. 28-29. The Lord Jesus was indicating that if someone is going to build a tower he must sit down and count the cost, for it is important that the building is finished. Throughout Luke's Gospel, the Son of God finishes every work to which He put His hand. In chapter 7, He raises to life the son of the widow of Nain. He took account of the widow's tears and, having raised the young man to life, He completed what He did by delivering the young man to his mother again. In chapter 8, He raises to life the daughter of Jairus. He did not stop by raising her to life but also said, 'Give her meat', Luke 8. 55. In chapter 9, there is the account of how the Lord Jesus dispossessed the young man of the demon at the foot of the mount of transfiguration. Matthew, Mark and Luke all give an account of this but only Luke tells us that having dispossessed the young man of the demon He delivered him to his father. Then, in the delightful parable of chapter 10, the Samaritan met the man half dead by the wayside, bound up his wounds and poured in the oil and the wine. He is seen gloriously completing His work in that he put him on his beast and took him to an inn. Then, in chapter 15, there is the parable of the shepherd and the lost sheep, the woman and the lost piece of silver. The Saviour is careful to point out that the shepherd went after the sheep until he found it. The woman searched diligently for the silver until she found it. Neither of them left their task incomplete or unfinished. In chapter 22, there is Luke's account of Peter's betrayal of the Lord Jesus. Luke is the only one who tells us that after Peter had betrayed Jesus the Lord turned and looked on Peter. Luke alone indicates that not only did the Lord Jesus tell Peter that he would betray Him but when Peter did in fact betray Him, our Saviour turned and looked on Peter. Peter went out and wept bitterly. Notice, too, that Matthew, Mark, Luke and John all tell us how Peter cut off the servant's ear in the garden but only Luke tells us how the Lord touched the servant's ear and healed it. This is that of which the kidney speaks; He perfected, He completed every work to which He put His hand.

God also required *the caul above the liver*. The Hebrew root means 'the superabundance of the glory'. This is precious and it would repay the time to go through Luke's Gospel observing the superabundance of the glory. In chapter 4, He is led of the Spirit into the wilderness and tempted of the devil. The result was that He returned in the power of the Spirit into Galilee and in this we may observe the superabundance of the glory. In chapter 9, He feeds the five thousand with the result that they were left with more food than they commenced with; after He had fed the multitude they gathered up of the fragments, twelve baskets. This is the superabundance of the glory. In chapter 23, they nailed our Saviour to the cross and He is heard to say, 'Father, forgive them; for they know not what they do', v. 34. This all bespeaks the thought of the superabundance of the glory. The caul above the liver was placed on the altar for God; He required it for Himself.

The portion given to the officiating priest

The officiating priest dealt with the sacrifice itself, with the blood of the sacrifice and the fat, as distinct from other priests. In the study of the tabernacle or the offerings, when the officiating priest is viewed, distinct from the priestly family, he speaks of our Lord Jesus Christ, and the priestly family speaks of the Church. On the occasion of the consecration of the priesthood, when Aaron was consecrated by himself, oil was poured upon him without the need of blood being sprinkled. This is because He speaks of our Lord Jesus Christ. There is no need for his being sprinkled by blood if he speaks of our Lord Jesus Christ. When Aaron was anointed together with the family the oil was sprinkled on them but when Aaron was anointed by himself, without blood, the oil was poured upon him in rich profusion. This is referred to in Psalm 133 when it speaks of the oil upon his head and upon his beard that ran down to the skirts of his garment. Aaron the high priest anointed by himself in his consecration speaks of Christ but when he is anointed with the family the oil is just sprinkled on him. John says concerning the Saviour, 'God giveth not the Spirit by measure unto him', John 3. 34; the oil was, as it were, poured on Him. It is interesting to observe that Luke tells us that when He was anointed with the Spirit, the Spirit of God descended in bodily form as of a dove. The thought in a body is that of completeness. However, when the Spirit of God came down on the day of Pentecost, He did not descend in bodily form but as cloven tongues of fire. The tongue is just a member of the body and this gives us to appreciate the distinction between Christ and His people, the high priest and the priestly family.

The portion that was given to the officiating priest was the right shoulder, Lev. 7. 33. The right shoulder speaks of strength of service. This was given to the officiating priest who speaks of Christ because none knew, as did the Son of God, the strength that was required to complete the service of God.

None of the ransomed ever knew,
How deep were the waters crossed;
Or how dark was the night that the Lord passed through
E'er He found His sheep that was lost.

The portion of the priestly family

To them there was given the breast of the animal, Lev. 7. 31. The breast, throughout God's word, always speaks of love and affection. The priestly family is symbolic of the Church; the Church feeds upon the breast of the sacrifice. In Ephesians chapter 5, the apostle tells us that 'Christ also loved the church, and gave himself for it', v. 25, and the Church feasts upon this, the love of Christ, for it enabled Him to give Himself for the Church.

The Israelite's portion

In chapter 7 verses 15-18, we learn that the flesh of the peace offering was given to the Israelite who brought the offering that he might feast upon it with his family. Notice this division: God got the inwards, the officiating priest the right shoulder, the priestly family the breast, the Israelite and his family the flesh.

The Israelite and his family speak of Israel, that nation which is going to share in the blessings of Calvary. It is a tremendous tragedy that there is that line of teaching being perpetuated today that would indicate that there is no future for Israel. Let us be assured that Israel as a nation will yet share in the fruits of the sacrifice of Calvary. In their feeding on the flesh, we learn that if the Church feeds on the love of Christ, Israel feeds on the mercy of God. Israel will yet be restored, according to Romans chapter 11, on the ground of sovereign mercy. 'I will have mercy on whom I will have mercy', Rom 9. 15. Mercy is an issue of love; God is merciful, because He is a God of love. God is 'rich in mercy, for his great love wherewith he loved us', Eph. 2. 4. If the Church feeds upon the love of Christ for her, Israel realizes that in the sovereign mercy of God, because of Calvary, she is restored to God, though her restoration is yet future.

God wanted the *inwards*, the suet, the kidneys and the caul above the liver. That which the human eye could not see God wanted placed on the altar for Him. This is most important. What the eye of God alone could see in Christ, the heart of God alone could appreciate. Remember His words from the open heavens as He is looking in, 'Thou art my beloved Son, in whom I am well pleased', Mark 1. 11.

Then, in Christ's portion as the Hebrew priest, was *the right shoulder*, strength for service. We shall never know what it meant to our Saviour to say in the garden of Gethsemane, 'Not as I will, but as thou wilt', Matt. 26. 39. In the garden of Gethsemane Christ was feeding on the right shoulder, taking hold of the strength that was necessary to carry out the will of God. Feeding upon it, He was heard to say, 'The cup which my Father hath given me, shall I not drink it?' John 18. 11.

Then, there is *the breast* of the animal. It is called the wave breast in chapter 7 because the breast of the animal was waved to and fro before the Lord. The breast of God's Son could be waved to and fro before the Lord for the Lord's pleasure and acceptance because there was nothing within His breast that would grieve His God. Each of us would have to take our stand alongside the publican in Luke chapter 18, smite ourselves on the breast and, not so much as looking up into heaven, say, 'God be merciful to me a sinner'. With regard to God's Son, however, His breast typically is waved before the Lord because there was nothing in it to grieve Him.

The flesh was given to the Israelite and his family that he might take it home and feed upon it in his home.

There were three occasions in which a peace offering might be offered. It might be offered on an occasion of thanksgiving, Lev. 7. 15, when God had shown to the Israelite some particular favour and mercy and he wanted to express his thankfulness. Again, it could be offered on the occasion of making a vow, v. 16, or it could be offered voluntarily. If an Israelite desired to make a vow to do something for God he was to give expression to the desire of his heart by bringing a peace offering. Also, the Israelite could bring a peace offering voluntarily without any particular mercy for which he wanted to be thankful and apart from the occasion of making a vow. He might just bring it out of a heart in tune with God. The three occasions on which it might be offered were thanksgiving, a vow or voluntarily.

Notice, however, that God allowed the Israelite to take the flesh of the peace offering to his home when he offered a peace offering of thanksgiving, that he might feed upon it in his own home with his family on the day that he had been to the altar. It was not to be eaten on the second day. If, however, he brought the peace offering on the occasion of making a vow or voluntarily God allowed him to take the flesh into his own home so that while at home with the family he might feed upon the flesh not only on the day that he had been to the altar but also on the second day. It was not to be eaten on the third day. Thus, when it was a vow or a voluntary offering God gave to the Israelite an extra day in which he could eat of the flesh of his peace offering in his home. This is important. In this God is taking into account the degree of devotion of the Israelite. God knew that if He had granted to an Israelite some particular mercy and they desired to be thankful, that did not call for any great degree of devotion. The least that God can expect from any one of us is that we be thankful. It does not demand any great degree of spirituality to be thankful and God took this into account with the Israelite. God did not want the Israelite to make the flesh of the peace offering a common meal, to partake of it in his home divorced from his visit to the altar. In other words, God did not desire that holy things should become common. Taking account of the increased degree of devotion when it was a vow or voluntary offering, God allowed the Israelite another day, accepting that he would eat it at home not as a common meal but still connected with his visit to the altar.

With many of God's people today holy things are becoming common. How often we hear unbecoming jocularity about texts in God's word, holy things becoming common. Perhaps we read the scriptures before we go to bed, not because we enjoy them but as a duty. Perhaps we give thanks for our meal but do not turn off the radio. Perhaps we come to the breaking of bread and we are more interested in the fashions that are there, than in the purpose of the gathering. Oftentimes the cup is going round and after an individual has partaken of the cup the rattle of money may be heard, indicating that even the cup has become a common thing, its deep significance forgotten. Scarcely has the meeting closed but there is an unbecoming din, laughter, conversation, and perhaps the showing of photographs. It seems that God's people can turn their back on the holiest in a few seconds, and there is the serious possibility of holy things becoming common.

God had restrictions on the eating of the flesh of the peace offering. In chapter 7 verse 19, all that are clean have to eat of it, indicating that only those who have been sanctified through faith in Christ Jesus must handle holy things. It is a serious thing for a person not sanctified through faith in Christ to handle holy things. In verse 20, no Israelite having his uncleanness upon him must eat of it, teaching us that we must never handle holy things if there is unjudged or unconfessed sin in the life. In verse 21, no Israelite who has touched any unclean thing, whether it was the uncleanness of man or of beast or abominable unclean thing, must eat of the flesh of the peace offering. In this we learn that if we tamper with evil and there is sin we must not handle holy things. If we do we can incur the judgement and the chastisement of God. The apostle Paul said, 'For if we would judge ourselves, we should not be judged', 1 Cor. 11. 31.

THE SIN OFFERING AND THE TRESPASS OFFERING

Leviticus 4

Chapter 4 begins with the statement, 'And the Lord spake unto Moses'. It has already been noted that this is one of the key statements of the book of Leviticus and each time that it occurs it indicates a new and a fresh revelation. This is the second time that this has occurred in the book of Leviticus. The first time was in chapter 1 verse 1 and thus we have one revelation covering chapters 1, 2 and 3. There is now another revelation at the commencement of chapter 4, because chapter 4 begins with a consideration of a different kind of offering. The burnt offering, the meal offering and the peace offering were voluntary offerings that ascended to the Lord as a sweet savour. In chapters 4, 5 and 6, we have the sin and the trespass offerings. These were not voluntary but obligatory and were not, largely speaking, sweet savour; these were non-sweet savour offerings. When an Israelite sinned, God did not leave it to him to offer his sin or trespass offering when he willed. God expected that the moment he became aware of his sin or his trespass he would feel obliged to offer his sin or his trespass offering. This is the reason for the new revelation.

There are four sections to be considered in chapters 4, 5 and 6.

Chapter 4 gives the account of the *sin offering* and account is taken of sins of ignorance. Verse 2 says, 'If a soul shall sin through ignorance against any of the commandments of the Lord concerning things which ought not to be done'.

This is a chapter of tremendous variety. There is variety in the offerers, in the animals that might be offered and in the mode of the offering of these various animals. In none of the offerings is there the variety that we have in the sin offering. All this is significant and heart-searching.

The different persons that might sin

The *priest* that is anointed might sin. Nadab and Abihu might be remembered as being anointed priests who sinned. The *whole congregation* might sin and the murmuring of the whole congregation in the wilderness is an example of this. A *ruler* might sin; the sin of King David with the wife of Uriah is a prime example. One of the *common people* might sin; Achan took goods from Jericho.

Not one of God's people, whatever their spiritual status, is immune from sinning. When God saves He gives a new nature but He does not take away the old nature. That new nature could not and did not improve the old nature, which believers will have with them as long as they are down here. It is always as capable of doing anything that ever it did and for that reason none of us is immune from sinning. The language of Paul is, 'Let him that thinketh he standeth take heed lest he fall', 1 Cor. 10. 12. This means that the moment a believer thinks that he is standing he is the most likely to fall. Invariably, it is in the very thing in which a person thinks he is strong that he falls. Those who by God's mercy are preserved are those who are so terribly conscious of their weakness.

The different animals that might be offered

A young bullock, a male kid or a female kid could be offered. The reason for this was that in the sin offering it is not just man's guilt viewed in relation to God's holiness but to man's responsibility and the relative position, or office, of the offender is taken into account. In Leviticus chapter 4, the sin offering is not offered to establish a relationship between a man and his God, as that relationship already exists. Rather, the sin offering is offered by a man whose communion with God has been disturbed, and when a man in relationship with God sins the gravity of his sin is assessed by the relative position or dignity of his office. The Lord provides that if the anointed priest sins he is to offer a young bullock but if it is one of the common people that sins he would accept from him a female kid.

When it comes to the establishment of relationship between the sinner and God we turn not to the book of Leviticus but to the book of Exodus. In Exodus chapter 12, there was in every house the same offering, the offering of a lamb. In Exodus chapter 30, there is, again, the establishment of relationship in the redemption of the life by the payment of the ransom money. It was the same for all; each had to pay a half shekel of silver and God made it clear that the rich must not pay any more nor the poor any less. In the matter of establishing relationship, it is man's guilt in relationship to God's holiness. Christians love to tell sinners as we preach the Gospel that the best need nothing less than Christ and, at the same time, He suffices for the worst. It is the same for all when it comes to the matter of salvation and the establishing of relationship between the sinner and God. In Leviticus chapter 4, however, men are already in relationship with God and if they sin their relative position is taken into account. In fact, it becomes a very serious matter. It is a serious matter for an ungodly person to sin, more serious for a child of God to sin and even more serious for a leader amongst God's people to sin. That lesson we learn in Leviticus chapter 4.

The different modes of offering the various sacrifices

When there was a sin offering for the priest, or the whole congregation, the blood was taken into the holy place. It was sprinkled seven times before the veil. Also, some of the blood was put upon the horns of the golden altar of incense and the rest of the blood was poured out at the base of the brazen altar. With regard to the flesh of this sin offering, if it was for the priest or the whole congregation the animal was taken outside the camp and the head, the legs, the skin and the dung were burned in a devouring fire. However, when it was one of the common people that sinned, or a ruler, the blood was never taken into the holy place but it was sprinkled on the horns of the brazen altar and poured out at its base. The flesh was not burned outside the camp but it was eaten by the priest and the male priests of the priestly family in a holy place.

When the priest that was anointed sinned, he sinned according to the sin of the people. Verse 3 says, 'If the priest that is anointed do sin according to the sin of the people'. In other words, the sin of the priest incriminated the people of God because he was their spiritual leader who wielded a tremendous influence upon God's people. When a spiritual leader sins there is the serious danger of his sin incriminating the people of God. Additionally, the anointed priest could sin and incriminate the people by his teaching. The priest was one whose lips kept knowledge, through whom God's people learned the ways of God. It was a serious matter for a man to sin who taught God's people, for he could sin according to the sin of the people.

Not a few brethren seek for position. Any man who appreciates the tremendous responsibilities attached to being a leader of God's people could never desire it without real exercise and a deep burden of heart. It is a serious matter; woe betide that leader amongst God's people who, by his teaching or his influence, leads the people of God into wrong paths. That becomes very clear in Leviticus chapter 4.

In connection with the offering of the sin offering for the anointed priest it is necessary to observe certain omissions. For instance, it does not say in connection with the anointed priest as it does with others, 'If he sin through ignorance'. He was a man whose lips kept knowledge because of his position as a man who knew the ways of God and it was not expected that such should sin ignorantly. It must not be thought that ignorance is any excuse or that ignorance lessens guilt. Ignorance can oftentimes increase guilt and so in His word God makes very little provision for the ignorance of His people. There is no cause for ignorance with such a book as we have.

Again, it does not say, 'If the thing be hid from his eyes'. There is no thought of a priest sinning that sin being hid from him and, at a later date, coming to his knowledge. The anointed priest was one who ministered in the sanctuary, before the veil, at the golden altar, in relation to the golden lampstand and the table of shewbread. His feet trod the holy place and it was not expected that a man who lived and served in the sanctuary in the presence of God could sin and the sin be hid from him. If there is anything going to a make a believer sensitive to sin, to those things that are grieving to God, it will be the cultivation of a sense of God's presence. Often God's people say that they do not see any harm in this or that thing in which they desire to be engaged. One who thinks like that knows very little of the presence of God, for one who lives in the company of God will never reason in that way. Rather, he will look to see if there is anything for God's glory in this or that. When believers reason from that standpoint many doubtful things are immediately solved for us. Those who live near to God are not only increasingly sensitive to the things that please God but they become increasingly sensitive to the things that grieve God. Thus, in connection with the priest, it does not speak of the thing being hid from him and eventually coming to his knowledge.

Further, it does not say after he has offered his sin offering that his sin would be forgiven him. The priest was a man who knew perfectly well that if, having sinned, he did what God told him to do God must forgive his sin. He did not need that assurance; all he needed to know was that he had done exactly as God had told him to do. As God's people we are never called upon to ask God to forgive us our sins. Rather, we are called upon to confess our sins, 'if we confess our sins He is faithful and just to forgive us our sins', 1 John 1. 9. It does not say, 'If we confess our sins, He is merciful and gracious to forgive us our sins', which is what we should expect. In fact, He is faithful to the blood of Christ and righteous because of it, in forgiving our sins. Confession is no half-hearted apology for having sinned; but having sinned, if we make the kind of confession that God our Father expects us to make, there is forgiveness immediately such a confession is made. We need not be assured of it; we need not to ask for it. All we need to do is obey, to carry out what God has told us in His word to do.

There are many other details that we must pass over in connection with the priest but we note that the blood was sprinkled before the veil, on the golden altar, and at the brazen altar. This is because the anointed priest ministered before these places. If he had sin in his life, every place that he touched in his service for God was affected by it. That principle still applies today. If there is unconfessed and unjudged sin in the life of the believer every place that he touches in his service for God is defiled by it.

We are told how that the head, the legs, the flesh, the skin and the dung of the animal was carried outside the camp and consumed; not on an altar, or on wood, but where the ashes were poured out. It is necessary to observe the different words for 'burning' which are used in relation to the offerings. For instance, in the burnt offering of chapter 1, the word for 'burning' means 'a slow burning'. It is a slow burning so as to cause incense of a sweet savour. The word for 'burning' in relation to the sin offering burned outside the camp is not a slow burning, but a quick burning, a devouring flame so as to put away. Thus, the priest that was anointed, having confessed his sin upon the head of a young bullock, saw its head with its legs, its flesh, its skin and its dung carried outside the camp and devoured quickly in a consuming flame. When he saw the animal, upon whose head he had confessed his sin, reduced to ashes he knew that his sin had been borne away and put out of sight. With the burnt offering, before the legs and the inwards were placed upon the altar they had to be washed, but there was no washing with this sin offering. The sacrifice was carried out as it was and burned in that devouring flame outside the camp. This may remind us of 2 Corinthians chapter 5 verse 21, 'For he hath made him to be sin for us, who knew no sin; that we might be made the righteousness of God in him'. For our Saviour, the very thought of His being the antitype of the sin offering reduced to ashes outside the camp, His being made sin, was what occasioned His agony, His exceeding sorrow,

His being sore troubled, His sweat, and His prostration in the garden of Gethsemane.

In connection with the sin offering, the inwards of the animal that was burned outside the camp were laid on the brazen altar and ascended as a sweet savour to God. There was a sweet savour in Christ as the sin offering when, in the Garden in His agony, sweat and sorrow the Lord Jesus contemplated being made sin. This is that wherein God found delight, even in the sin offering. Despite its awfulness, our Saviour said, 'Not as I will, but as thou wilt', Matt. 26. 39. That brought pleasure to God; here the inwards were placed on the altar, a heart devoted to the will of God and prepared to carry out the work that God gave him to do.

If the ruler or one of the common people sinned, the blood of their sin offering was not taken into the holy place but it was sprinkled on the horns of the brazen altar and poured out at its base. This is because the ruler or the common people never went any further than the brazen altar and thus that is all that was affected by their sin.

As far as the flesh of the sin offering of the ruler or the common people was concerned, we are told in chapter 6 verse 26 that it was eaten by the officiating priest in a holy place. When the officiating priest is viewed as distinct from the priestly family he speaks of Christ. This makes me to appreciate how that Christ not only bore the wrath of God for our sins on that shameful tree, thereby setting us free, but each time that we sin He feels it up there, so to speak, in the holy place, in the very presence of God. Additionally, however, that same flesh was eaten by the male priests in a holy place. This tells me that priestly men among God's people feel the sin of God's people in the sanctuary. In connection with the peace offering, the Israelite could take the flesh of the peace offering into his home and eat it there with his family, but in connection with the sin offering the male priests could not take the flesh home. God says, 'You'll eat of it, but only in a holy place'. All too often today, God's people eat of the flesh of other people's sin offerings in their homes and not in a holy place. It is always a dreadful tragedy when God's people love to gossip over the sins and failures of others. Shame on us if we do! If our brethren sin and fail we should certainly never gossip over it, if we are in touch with God, but we will feel it as our High Priest feels it in the very presence of God Himself.

We shall briefly consider some principles in connection with *the trespass offering*. In this offering, whether it is a trespass in the holy things or a trespass against the Lord, there was, in the trespass, an element of wilfulness. For instance, in chapter 6, we read how that an Israelite might tell a lie to his neighbour in relationship to that which his neighbour has given to keep for him. There were no banks in those days and if an Israelite was going on a long journey he would leave his valuable possessions with a neighbour. It may be that during his absence the neighbour appropriates that which was left in his custody and, on the return of the Israelite, the neighbour tells a lie concerning it. He might claim, for instance, that someone had stolen it. In this case there was a wilful trespass in that he told his neighbour a lie. In the same section we learn how an Israelite might go so far as to deceive his neighbour. These were wilful sins having the character of a trespass.

In **chapter 5 verses 1-13,** there is a peculiar section wherein *a trespass offering was offered for a sin offering*. In this section, which has given not a little trouble to students of the offerings, the particular sin that is committed has an element of ignorance and an element of wilfulness. Chapter 5 verse 1 says, 'And if a soul sin, and hear the voice of swearing, and is a witness, whether he hath seen or known of it; if he do not utter it, then he shall bear his iniquity'. The word 'swearing' really is 'adjuration' and the thought is of being adjured as a witness. The Israelite has not committed the offence, as he only saw it or heard about it; in that he is ignorant. However, when the time comes that he is adjured to be a witness and he refuses to testify then he is morally as guilty as the culprit himself. Thus, there was an element of ignorance in that he did not commit the offence and there was an element of wilfulness in that he refused to testify.

In verse 2, an Israelite might touch the uncleanness of the dead body, of a wild beast, a domesticated animal or a creeping thing. He would not do this wittingly but ignorantly. Leviticus chapter 11 makes provision for the Israelite who touches the uncleanness of these bodies in that he could wash himself and be clean, but if he has neglected this washing then he must bring a trespass offering for a sin offering. The element of ignorance is that unwittingly he touched these dead bodies, but the element of wilfulness is that he did not avail himself of the water of cleansing. Accordingly, he must offer a trespass offering for a sin offering.

In verse 4, an Israelite might make a rash vow. It is the thought of an Israelite foolishly and inconsiderately through ignorance making a vow not realizing all that was involved, but he wilfully refuses to keep his vow. Once more there is an element of ignorance and an element of wilfulness. David made a rash vow that he would kill Nabal. Jephthah made a rash vow that he would sacrifice to the Lord whatsoever should meet him.

Accordingly, there are, in chapter 4, sins of ignorance and, in chapter 5 verses 1-13, sins of rashness.

The third section, from **chapter 5 verses 14-19,** speaks of *a trespass offering relative to a trespass in the holy things*. An Israelite might trespass in the holy things by keeping back any of the offerings that God required of him, or by eating of the tithes within his gate, or by failing to sanctify the firstborn of his males. In all of these things, he was trespassing against the law. Thus, he had to bring a ram according to Moses' valuation; he had to make amends for the trespass he had committed and add a fifth part more by way of compensation. Having done this, he offered his trespass offering and the matter was right with God. The idea in a trespass is really that of defrauding. A man can defraud God and his neighbour. The question is asked in the Old Testament, 'Will a man rob God?' Mal. 3. 8. We also may rob God. If I am improperly absent from the breaking of bread on the first day of the week, when God rightly expects from me His portion, I rob God. Or, if I am present but my basket is empty and I have nothing to offer, I rob God. If I belong to Christ and yet give so much time that I should be devoting to the interests of the Lord to pleasure, habits and hobbies, I rob God. Indeed, there are so many ways in which we as God's people could rob Him. If this has been true in our lives, let us make an honest confession to Him wherein we have robbed Him; this is making amends. Let us also pay the fifth part more compensation by telling God, in all sincerity, that, in the few days that lie between now and His coming again, we shall be better men and women for Him than we were in the past. The result will be that God will be enriched, we shall be blessed and all God's people will also be blessed in turn.

The fourth section is **chapter 6 verses 1-7** and here there is *a trespass offering not in the holy things, and not primarily against the Lord, but an Israelite trespassing against his neighbour.* Thus, there could be two kinds of trespass, or sins of wilfulness: a trespass against the Lord and a trespass against one's neighbour.

The Israelite might defraud his brother. He might lie unto him or deceive him in the kind of things that are enumerated for us in chapter 6. The Lord Jesus made it clear that we cannot treat our brethren as we like; we must see to it that we render to our brethren the loyalty and fidelity that is their due. Many of the Lord's people (and I speak to my own heart) do not maintain an upright, sincere, faithful relationship with their brethren. They are nice to their face but quite different behind their back. If that is the case then they are defrauding their brother.

The Israelite had to make amends to his neighbour and having done so pay a fifth part more by way of compensation. Then, he had to bring his ram for a trespass offering. I learn that if I have wronged a brother or a sister I should make an honest confession of what I have done to make amends. In addition, I should pay to them a fifth part more compensation by telling them, 'I will be a better brother to you in the future than I have been in the past'.

Also, confession must be made to God the Father. Here is a principle. It is not enough to say that you have put that matter right with God; the fact of the matter is that it has never been put right with God if it has not been put right with your brother.

Every kind of sin that any of God's people might commit (sins of ignorance, sins of rashness or sins of wilfulness) is covered. God does not condone these things but God so desires the communion of His people that, should they sin ignorantly, rashly or wilfully, He has made provision that their communion might be restored. It must not be thought that the fact that God made provision meant that an Israelite could sin as He willed any more than the fact that God had made provision for us in the present day means that we can sin when and as we will. In fact, if any professing believer can sin habitually and without a conscience a question arises as to whether such has ever been saved at all. John says, 'If any man sin' not, 'when any man sin'. 'If any man sin, we have an advocate with the Father, Jesus Christ the righteous', 1 John 2. 1. This should cause us to appreciate how much our God desires the communion of His people.